OXFORD GEOGRAPHICAL AND
ENVIRONMENTAL STUDIES

Editors: Gordon Clark, Andrew Goudie, and Ceri Peach

GLOBALIZATION AND INTEGRATED AREA DEVELOPMENT IN EUROPEAN CITIES

ALSO PUBLISHED BY
OXFORD UNIVERSITY PRESS
IN THE OXFORD GEOGRAPHICAL
AND ENVIRONMENTAL STUDIES SERIES

The New Middle Class and the Remaking of the Central City
David Ley

Culture and the City in East Asia
Won Bae Kim, Mike Douglass, Sang-Chuel Choe,
and Kong Chong Ho (eds.)

Energy Structures and Environmental Futures in Europe
Torleif Haugland, Helge Ole Bergesen,
and Kjell Roland

Homelessness, Aids, and Stigmatization
Lois Takahashi

Dynamics of Regional Growth in Europe
Social and Political Factors
Andrés Rodríguez-Pose

Island Epidemics
Andrew Cliff, Peter Haggett,
and Matthew Smallman-Raynor

Pension Fund Capitalism
Gordon L. Clark

Cultivated Landscapes of Native North America
William E. Doolittle

Indigenous Land Management in West Africa
An Environmental Balancing Act
Kathleen Baker

Class, Ethnicity, and Community in Southern Mexico
Oaxaca's Peasantries
Colin Clarke

Globalization and Integrated Area Development in European Cities

Frank Moulaert

in collaboration with Pavlos Delladetsima,
Jean-Cédric Delvainquière, Christophe Demazière,
Arantxa Rodriguez, Serena Vicari and
Marian Martinez Yeste

OXFORD
UNIVERSITY PRESS

OXFORD

UNIVERSITY PRESS

Great Clarendon Street, Oxford OX2 6DP

Oxford University Press is a department of the University of Oxford.
It furthers the University's objective of excellence in research, scholarship,
and education by publishing worldwide in

Oxford New York

Athens Auckland Bangkok Bogotá Buenos Aires Calcutta
Cape Town Chennai Dar es Salaam Delhi Florence Hong Kong Istanbul
Karachi Kuala Lumpur Madrid Melbourne Mexico City Mumbai
Nairobi Paris São Paulo Shanghai Singapore Taipei Tokyo Toronto Warsaw

and associated companies in Berlin Ibadan

Oxford is a registered trade mark of Oxford University Press
in the UK and in certain other countries

Published in the United States
by Oxford University Press Inc., New York

© Frank Moulaert 2000

British Library Cataloguing in Publication Data

Data available

Library of Congress Cataloging in Publication Data

Globalization and integrated area development in European cities /
Frank Moulaert in collaboration with Pavlos Delladetsima . . . [et al.].
p. cm.—(Oxford geographical and environmental studies)
Includes bibliographical references and index.
1. Economic development projects—Europe—Case studies.
2. Cities and towns—Europe—Case studies.
3. Globalization—Europe—Case studies.
4. Competition, International.
I. Moulaert, Frank. II. Delladetsima, Pavlos, III. Series.
HC240.9.E44 G55 2000 307.76'094—dc21 00–040072

ISBN 0–19–924113–9

1 3 5 7 9 10 8 6 4 2

Typeset by Hope Services (Abingdon) Ltd.
Printed in Great Britain
on acid-free paper by
T.J. International
Padstow, Cornwall

EDITORS' PREFACE

Geography and environmental studies are two closely related and burgeoning fields of academic inquiry. Both have grown rapidly over the past two decades. At once catholic in its approach and yet strongly committed to a comprehensive understanding of the world, geography has focused upon the interaction between global and local phenomena. Environmental studies, on the other hand, has shared with the discipline of geography an engagement with different disciplines addressing wide-ranging environmental issues in the scientific community and the policy community of great significance. Ranging from the analysis of climate change and physical processes to the cultural dislocations of postmodernism these two fields of inquiry have been in the forefront of attempts to comprehend transformations taking place in the world, manifesting themselves at a variety of separate but interrelated spatial scales.

The 'Oxford Geographical and Environmental Studies' series aims to reflect this diversity and engagement. Our aim is to publish the best original research in the two related fields and in doing so, to demonstrate the significance of geographical and environmental perspectives for understanding the contemporary world. As a consequence, its scope is international and ranges widely in terms of its topics, approaches, and methodologies. Its authors will be welcomed from all corners of the globe. We hope the series will assist in redefining the frontiers of knowledge and build bridges within the fields of geography and environmental studies. We hope also that it will cement links with topics and approaches that have originated outside the strict confines of these disciplines. Resulting studies contribute to frontiers of research and knowledge as well as representing individually the fruits of particular and diverse specialist expertise in the traditions of scholarly publication.

Gordon Clark
Andrew Goudie
Ceri Peach

Voor Albert, vriend en inspirator

PREFACE

This book is neither the work of a single author, nor an edited collective volume. It is a collective book that has been written by six authors, involved in theoretical and case-study work related to its general theme, i.e. Integrated Area Development as a specific form of socially innovative local development in the era of globalization. As the project leader and the theoretical guide of this work, it has been my task to rewrite all the chapters.

This collective authorship has an important symbolic value: like the innovative forms of collaboration in the integrated area development model defended in the book, authorship solidarity is a type of social capital that is essential in order to write about a multidimensional social subject such as local development itself.

The research that led to this book was mainly funded by the European Commission DG V, the French DATAR and the French national science foundation CNRS (IFRESI), and the Agence de Développement et d'Urbanisme (Lille). But in addition to these institutional acknowledgements, thanks are due to all our colleagues who participated in the research on local development as a strategy to combat poverty in the European Union (European Union, Poverty III). We especially want to mention Rosemarie Sackmann and Hartmut Häussermann who studied Hamburg and Rostock, as well as Ricardo Alaez and Jesus Ferreiro who investigated development dynamics in Bilbao and Girona. The working papers, which they wrote in 1992 and 1994, were a valuable starting-point for the study of the development strategies in these localities.

We wish to thank Ulrich Häntsch, Karin Schmalriede from the Johann Daniel Lawaetz-Stiftung, Andreas Schubert from the Rostock City authorities, and Eddy Cop from the Antwerp City authorities. They provided data and gave critical comments to the case studies on Hamburg, Rostock, and Antwerp.

Many thanks also to Phil Haddock who let us exploit his native linguistic instinct, Kourosh Saljoghi who offered his technical skills for the production of the figures, Vincent Wenquin, for his photography of *La Forêt Humaine* and Michel Noléo who, as a final editor in Lille, survived my bad temper.

F.M.

Lille
19 November 1999

ACKNOWLEDGEMENTS

The authors wish to thank :

Pion Ltd. for permission to publish as Chapter 3 of this book an updated and extended version of F. Moulaert, 'Rediscovering Spatial Inequality in Europe: Building Blocks for an Appropriate "Regulationist" Framework', *Society and Space*, 14 (1996), 155–79.

   Presses Universitaires du Québec for letting us translate and adapt as part of Chapter 4 of this book F. Moulaert, Jean-Cédric Delvainquière, and Pavlos Delladetsima, 'Les Rapports sociaux dans le développement local: le rôle des mouvements sociaux', in J.-L. Klein, P.-A. Tremblay, and H. Dionne (eds.), *Au-delà du néolibéralisme. Quel rôle pour les mouvements sociaux?* (1997).

The authors

CONTENTS

THE AUTHORS

Frank Moulaert is **Professor of Economics** and Associate Dean for International Relations at the Faculty of Economics and Sociology, University of Science and Technology of Lille (France). He is a research co-ordinator at IFRESI-CNRS, Lille. His main research interests are urban analysis, regional and local development, and institutional economics. He co-ordinates several European networks providing research and education in these fields. He has published seven edited volumes and three books, as well as journal articles in *Environment and Planning*, *Journal of Post-Keynesian Economics*, *Urban Studies*, *Progress in Planning*, *International Journal of Urban and Regional Research*, and *Society and Space.* With Allen Scott he has recently published *Cities, Enterprises and Society on the Eve of the 21st Century* (London: Pinter, 1997).

Christophe Demazière is **Associate Professor of Planning** at Centre d'Etudes Supérieures d'Aménagement of the University of Tours (France). He was trained as a spatial economist at the University of Lille, with a doctorate on regional and urban dynamics and development strategies in north-west Europe. At the University of Tours, he is a researcher both at Ville-Société-Territoire and the Maison des Sciences de la Ville. He has done research on urban regeneration in France and Belgium, and more recently on development policies and tools in French regions. He is the author, editor, or co-editor of three books, including *Local Economic Development in Europe and the Americas* (London: Mansell , 1996, co-edited with Patricia Wilson).

Jean-Cédric Delvainquière is **'chargé d'études'** at the Ministry of Culture in Paris, France. He is finishing his Ph.D. dissertation on local development strategies in the urban region of Valenciennes. Together with Frank Moulaert and Christophe Demazière he worked at IFRESI (CNRS) on a number of studies for the European Commission on Local Economic Development in Disintegrated Areas: A Pro-active Strategy Against Poverty in Europe and published several articles on this topic.

Pavlos Marinos A. Delladetsima, Associate Professor of Geography, teaches Urban and Regional Planning and Land Policy at the University of the Aegean in Greece (Department of Geography). He was a Human Capital and Mobility research fellow (EEC) at IFRESI, Lille (France). He has also worked as a researcher at the National Technical University of Athens. P. M. Delladetsima has been involved in comparative European research on local development and has co-ordinated and participated in numerous research programmes on planning and local development for the European Community/Union. With L. Leontidou he has published 'Athens' in *European Planning Systems and Property Markets* (McGreal, S. and Berry, J., F. & F.N. Spon, 1995).

Arantxa Rodriguez, Associate Professor at the Faculty of Economics of the University of the Basque Country (Bilbao-Spain) focuses her research on the dynamics of socio-economic restructuring and spatial development planning in the Basque Country. Since the mid-1980s, she has been directly involved in the production of several urban plans in the Basque Country. She has also carried out research on the articulation between physical, functional, and economic planning and local economic development strategies. Among her recently published work are: 'Nuevas políticas y nuevos instrumentos para la revitalización metropolitana', in *Encuentros de Desarrollo Local y Empleo* (Coruña, 1997), and 'Planning the Revitalisation of an Old Industrial City: Urban Policy Innovations in Metropolitan Bilbao', in *Local Economic Development in Europe and the Americas* (London: Mansell, 1996, edited by C. Demazière and P. Wilson).

Serena Vicari Haddock is **Associate Professor in Sociology** at the University of Pavia (Italy). Since 1994 she has been secretary-treasurer of the Research Committee on Sociology of Urban and Regional Development of the International Sociological Association. Her fields of interest are urban development, technology, and society. Her current research projects are: urban redevelopment and social polarization in the city, civic networking, and virtual community. Among her recent publications in English is 'The Political Economy of Urban Regimes: A Comparative Perspective' (in collaboration with P. Kantor and H. V. Savitch), *Urban Affairs Review* (Jan. 1997).

Marian Martinez Yeste recently graduated in European Studies and New Technology from the University of East London (1997). Together with Frank Moulaert she has worked at IFRESI-CNRS in Lille (France) on Local Economic Development and Innovation of High Technology Consultancy Firms within the Nord-Pas-de Calais region.

LIST OF FIGURES

LIST OF TABLES

Introduction

Metropolitan cities must seek to occupy a privileged place in the new global division of labour, by complying with the laws of the 'global economy'. This is the only way to benefit from the new prosperity offered by international capital, to create new jobs and to rescue significant parts of urban population from poverty.

T.F.P.

This book seeks to break with this discourse in several ways. First, it argues that the universe of cities is much larger than the world of metropolises. Relationships between *metropolitan* cities and the global economy are the main topic in the literature on the impact of globalization on cities. But these relationships are so specific that few lessons can be drawn for the future of smaller cities. The book thus explores the interaction between globalization dynamics and a diversified array of cities. Second, global economic strategies sign away the social, ecological, and possibly the economic future of society all over the world. Some authors portray economic globalization as an advanced stage of neo-colonialism, practised not by national states but by corporate capital. The strategies implemented by the latter cause dreadful effects on Third World countries, old industrial nations and regions, cities and urban neighbourhoods. Globalization is not a new social agenda for a better planet, but a fierce leap forward in uneven development dynamics, and we believe it is scientifically and politically crucial to expose this aspect of globalization. Third, despite the gloomy picture of the impact of economic globalization on cities, this outcome is not inevitable: other strategic opportunities than coping with global trends are available to urban development agents pursuing local development.

The topic of the book is socially innovative local development in the context of globalization dynamics. The book develops a new multidisciplinary approach to the study of local development and attempts to answer the following questions:

- What is the real impact of globalization dynamics on cities and local communities?
- Does the global economy leave room for local development strategies and policies?

- Can local development programmes conciliate economic, social, and ecological agendas?
- Do existing local governance systems work in favour of local socio-economic development?

It is important to point out from the beginning that the focus of analysis and strategy selected for this book is that of the local community. The role of other spatial scales is mainly evaluated from a local stance, but this does not mean that the regional, national, or international (European) are less relevant scales of intervention for local development. When we argue in favour of Integrated Area Development, this also means the integration of the various spatial levels of analysis and action. And when governance and global regulation are examined, this is done with the absolute conviction that without national and international built-in guarantees, even the best among local development concepts will find it difficult to succeed. In this respect, national social policy aimed at reducing social inequality and exclusion (minimum income guarantees, democratic educational systems) and world governance favouring ecological and social justice among nations and peoples are essential to make socially innovative development work at the local level.

The book shows that Regulation Theory can be applied at the local level. Uncritical connoisseurs of this theory easily argue that regulation theory is a macro-economic theory, with little or no use at the local level. However, these scholars confuse macro and societal dynamics, the latter being equally relevant but taking different institutional forms at various spatial and social scales. Authors such as Jamie Peck, Adam Tickell, Nicholas Low, Danièle Leborgne, Bob Jessop, Alain Lipietz, Erik Swyngedouw, Hughes Sachter, and others have shown sufficiently well that regulation theory is a useful tool for local development analysis. We develop further the argument and apply this theoretical and methodological tool to the analysis of local development in a diversified sample of European localities.

The empirical material on which the book is based comes from five years of theoretical and empirical research into the relationship between social exclusion and the role of local development strategies. Localities have been researched at two levels. Twenty-nine localities of various plumages are covered in a general way according to the characteristics of their economic dynamics, socio-economic disintegration, regulation, and governance. Among these twenty-nine, six metropolitan areas (Antwerp, Bilbao, Charleroi, Gerona, Hamburg, Rostock) are examined in greater detail. Their development trajectories and experiences with alternative forms of development are depicted, compared, and evaluated. This two-level analysis is necessary to cover both aspects of empirical research using the regulation approach: the structural (or should we say the generic?) character of development dynamics that can be abstracted from the main features of the development trajectories in the twenty-nine localities; and the specificity of each local development experience which is reflected in the detail provided in each of the six urban experiences.

Readers familiar with regulation theory could skip the first part of Chapter 3. From section 3.2.2 onwards this theory is presented as an innovative framework for the study of local development, and this same framework is applied in the empirical research covered in Chapters 4 and 5.

1

Explaining the Tension: Global Competition, Social Exclusion, and Local Renaissance

This chapter explores different aspects of the relationship between the contemporary exclusion and development problems of inner cities in Western Europe on the one hand, and the socio-economic crisis that has been haunting the European continent since the middle of the 1970s on the other. Complementary and conflicting explanations of local crises or particular forms of global crises are examined and confronted with redevelopment strategies practised by local governments and development agents. The neo-liberal awakening and its new economic policy (NEP) are severely criticized and more support for socio-economic initiatives serving basic human needs is called for.

1.1 Problems of urban districts and neighbourhoods: an appraisal

Neighbourhoods of large cities, and especially their inner cities, i.e. the older, often more historical and centrally located neighbourhoods of larger cities, follow cycles of economic growth and decline. Depending on their role in the urban economy and society, these neighbourhoods may gain or lose in prosperity and status. Their populations may become richer or poorer, their social structure more or less polarized, their physical environment up or downgraded, etc. Today, if an inner city is considered to be problematic, this usually means that it combines many features of deprivation. Basic needs of social groups and citizens may be alienated: income to provide for basic goods and services, local education and training opportunities, quality housing and living environment, access to a democratic political system, security, and creative interaction with other parts of the urban society. The last refers to at least three dimensions of integration within urban society. Geographically, it means constructive relationships with other neighbourhoods in the city and with the larger urban region. Socio-economically, it involves access to the urban labour-market, the production and distribution system, and the financial system. And politically it implies that the neighbourhood's political demands find democratic expression and obtain access to the decision-making process of the urban society as a whole.

There is a notable concentration of basic needs in specific neighbourhoods. For the cities we examine in greater detail in Chapter 5 (Antwerp, Hamburg, Rostock, Girona, Charleroi, Bilbao) these neighbourhoods can be identified in a statistically significant way as areas in which the basic needs of significant segments of the population are denied. As an illustration, let us look at Fig. 1.1 which shows a map of Hamburg. Hamburg contains a number of neighbourhoods with a high percentage of social assistance recipients. These neighbourhoods are in general clustered near the city centre, and in particular Wilhelmsburg, Billstedt, and the most central smaller districts reach a poverty rate of over 14 per cent.

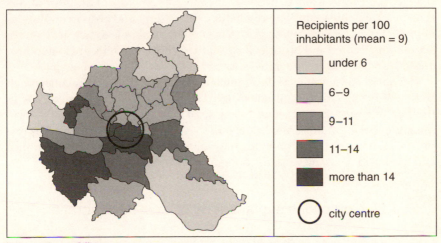

Source: Lawaetz Stiftung.

Fig. 1.1. Recipients of social assistance in Hamburg 1995
Source: Lawaetz-Stiftung.

However, it would be misleading to focus only on the concentration of social problems in particular neighbourhoods. Some studies argue that forms of so-called 'new poverty', affecting 'new' groups of poor, are ubiquitous in the city: the skilled unemployed (e.g. unemployed managers and engineers); people affected psychologically by the pressure of the socio-economic system or the lack of access to democratic control; workers who drop out of the work-process because of stress, and who are out of step with production norms and the way work is organized; potential welfare beneficiaries unable to cope with the paternalistic style of the welfare bureaucracy who choose to 'quit' and take to begging in the streets; and the homeless who are increasingly found in all layers of society (Kazepov and Zajczyk 1997).

Deprivation of basic rights, even when concentrated in certain neighbourhoods, involves the city as a whole, to the extent that the city is struggling for a
place in the new international and national order, for new development opportunities, and socio-political stability. The problems of groups and neighbourhoods are a reflection of hardship for the entire city as the pressure on different
structures and institutions within the city rises when poverty and deprivation
among one or more urban groups or areas increase. These problems mean a
structural challenge to local governance, policy, and politics. Conservative
forces seek to preserve the old balance between urban social groups, reflecting
periods of past or declining prosperity and social well-being, while new social
forces tend to replace or transform failing traditional civil institutions such as
party machines, unions, or even churches.

Attempts to explain the causes of socio-economic decline, deprivation, and
spatial disintegration and to propose possible solutions are at the heart of current political discussions. We present the explanations and proposed solutions
dominating the debate, but we also make an unmistakable choice in favour of
a multidimensional and historically grounded approach to local development
analysis and defend an integrated strategy in favour of 'local renaissance'.

This enriched view of local development also requires a broader conceptual-
ization of the dynamics of urban society. The identification of civil society as
the grey area between market and state is not sufficient for an attempt to scru-
tinize the social dynamics and leadership that produce urban change. The role
of new cultural, social, economic, and political actors needs to be identified
and located in the framework of contemporary urban governance.

1.2. Competing explanations of local disintegration

Competing explanations of local disintegration and social deprivation range
from straightforward arguments about inflexible labour-markets to the failure
of local development policies. The emphasis placed on the regional and local
level varies according to the explanatory framework.

1.2.1. Inflexible labour-markets

This explanation identifies the inflexible behaviour of labour-market partici-
pants and the public sector as the main cause of social exclusion. In a period of
economic restructuring, capital and production equipment should be used to
their full capacity and, to this purpose, the deployment of labour should be
rendered more flexible. This means that public regulation of the labour-
market should be mild mannered, enabling flexible working hours and wages,
reduced social protection, and increased human mobility so that more jobs can
be created at spatially equal capital and competitive labour cost. A dampening
effect on labour cost can be expected from workers and job seekers abandon-

ing their 'Fordist' or 'corporatist' attitude towards work and becoming available to enter less protected job positions.

The public sector is pinpointed as the cause of labour-market failure: the market fails to absorb job seekers because public regulation has crystallized labour-market behaviour. Unfortunately, because of its lack of historical memory, this neo-liberal view of labour-market mechanisms omits to mention that public regulation in the labour-market was at least partly a response to market failure during previous economic cycles. For example, Fordist labour-market policy, by supporting the purchasing power of workers and dismissed labourers, was meant to protect capital and labour from the volatility of a market drifting on the waves of growth trends and business cycles.

The flexibility/inflexibility argument is not very clear on the role of spatial differences in labour-markets. According to this theoretical perspective, unemployment and exclusion problems are expected to be worst in urban economies with rigid labour-markets, and flexible labour-markets are presented as a necessary ingredient of the New (Urban) Economic Policy.

1.2.2. Restructuring the Fordist economy

This is a historical explanation of socio-economic exclusion and deprivation. Both the prosperity and decline of national and regional economies are explained in terms of long-term growth patterns and national–regional economic specialization (Boyer and Mistral 1983). A distinction is often made between the Fordist (late 1940s–mid-1970s) and pre-Fordist growth periods. The Fordist economy is the national or regional economy that was basically driven by so-called Fordist leading sectors (automobile, chemicals, electrical domestic appliances, etc.) and a so-called Keynesian welfare state. When in the 1970s the economic engines of these sectors began to sputter, the regions which housed them on their territory became victims of economic stagnation and decline; but the regions with so-called pre-Fordist sectors (coal and steel, metal industry, glass, and shipyards, etc.) suffered even more badly. The continuing economic slackness of the 1980s struck the last and mortal blow to these industries. It transformed areas which for a very long period had been battling back against complete regression into manufacturing graveyards (see, for example, the debates in the context of RETI i.e. Régions Européennes de Tradition Industrielle in the 1980s).

In contrast to the previous explanation, spatial differentiation is quite clear: the uneven fate of regions and cities is explained in terms of their sector mix, their embeddedness in the Fordist economy, and their relationship to the national centres of political decision-making.

1.2.3. Technological innovation without redistribution

Local socio-economic disintegration is often presented as a direct or indirect consequence of radical technological innovation. In the footsteps of the economics of innovation literature analysing the consequences of the third or fourth 'industrial revolution', it is explained how firms can only survive the branding of technological competition through process and product innovations using computing and communications technology and other revolutionary basic technologies in the field of bio-engineering, sensor techniques, multi-media, etc. Firms applying these innovations successfully will increase or maintain their market share but unless their growth rates are significant their employment figures will decline dramatically. Given the deflationary climate caused by immediate massive unemployment following the first oil crisis, the drop in effective demand due to massive employment restructuring and the strict monetary policy, not enough new jobs were created to offset job losses arising from rationalization (Moulaert and Vandenbroucke 1983).

According to this approach, the macro-economic climate reinforces micro-economic dynamics. During the 1980s in the developed industrial nations the policy focus shifted from redistribution to the reinforcement of private and innovative capital. No measures were taken to transform the Fordist distribution mechanisms into post-Fordist redistribution tools. This meant that the localities with the most 'ancient' industrial systems were severely affected by product and process innovations, often resulting in the closing down of entire industries, the mushrooming of poverty, and the degradation of entire districts.

1.2.4. Globalization and the free-rider's prospect

This explanation combines the previous three theoretical views with the well-known globalization thesis, to which we return extensively in Chapter 2. This thesis proclaims that economic restructuring dynamics based on global finance, international corporate strategy, and complete liberalization of trade flows, will in a first phase cause high unemployment and structural imbalances in the labour-market, because of a lack of appropriate skills and mobility in human capital. In a second phase, however, global competition will lead to a modern and internationally integrated economy in which cities and regions that apply the New Economic Policy (NEP), i.e. that improve their physical environment (e.g. large-scale urban redevelopment projects), innovate their capital stock, train their labour force, extend their trade networks, foster a dynamic socio-cultural life, etc., will become very successful. But other cities that seek to improve their situation according to some local endogenous logic, and believe they can determine their own destiny as free riders of global capitalism, will perpetuate their history of economic disaster.

1.2.5. Local decline and (re)development potential

This view, which is at the heart of this book, argues that although structural crisis mechanisms, micro-economic innovation strategies, and globalization dynamics play a significant part in explaining structural exclusion mechanisms, much of the harm of socio-economic exclusion could have been avoided if different development practice and policy models had been employed. The New Economic Policy, when applied exclusively, can be as much a cause of crisis as the rationalization of old industrial sectors is itself (Cox 1995). NEP shows little respect for the socio-economic and socio-cultural history of cities, and constitutes a roadblock for development prospects based on local endogenous potential. The global economy leaves more space for local socio-political choices and creativity than the globalization thesis suggests. This space is in fact strongly determined by local governance dynamics, as we will see in Chapter 5.

1.3. Competing solutions

Analysing the causes of social exclusion and suggesting policies for overcoming them are closely related exercises. To compare policies effectively, one must confront their underlying analytical backbones. In this section, we summarize various views of economic policy, their ideological roots or orientation, and their (potential or effective) impact at a regional and urban level.

1.3.1. The global economy and national economic policy

A national economic policy that adopts the globalization thesis is aiming simultaneously at promoting the global economy and adapting national economic mechanisms to the terms of the global economy. Promoting the global economy means mainly liberalizing trade and capital flows (Altvater 1997). In theory, this would also mean free migration of labour. However, it turns out that, since the rise of globalization, restrictions on the free movement of workers and especially their families have become quite strict. One could in fact say with Russell King (1993*b*) that the nature of international migration has changed towards a stricter family reunification, selective labour migration, and war- and conflict-led political refugee policies. The adaptation of national mechanisms to the global economy mainly means deregulation of the economy, especially the flexibilization of labour-markets and the privatization of state-owned enterprises and public services. Certain competencies of the public sector, especially in the field of trade and capital regulation, have been ceded to international regulatory agencies, whereas others are increasingly left to regional and local authorities, which in the present economic situation seem to be better attuned to the interests of the private sector (see Moulaert *et al.* 1999).

The negative social and environmental consequences of these policies are easily demonstrated. In the field of labour relations, the threat of multilateral social dumping has become real and has created an international environment in which social progress is only possible in those production sectors with

significant productivity growth (Cuyvers and Rayp 1997). Especially outside
Europe (the USA is leading here) promising environmental policies are relaxed
to favour national competitiveness (Faber 1998). The social consequences of
these policies have been devastating. The loss of control over transnational
capital by the national states, with no effective *social* supranational regulatory
structures established, emasculates the national capacity to compensate for
social polarization in labour and housing markets, in the distribution of
income and wealth, and in the environmental and effective democratic content
of local well-being. Entire regions (perhaps even a whole continent as in the
case of Africa) are being excluded from the benefits of globalization and their
environment and health condition (cf. Aids in Africa) has been irreparably
damaged. At a national level, the revival of private-sector logic has replaced
the public interest by private waste generation, the continued destruction of
the environment (with the food chain as the new favourite target area), and the
reproduction of poverty.

1.3.2. New Economic Policy at the urban level

The New Economic Policy at a local level is completely in tune with the 'liberal'
stance supporting the globalization thesis. A cocktail of large-scale urban
development projects (high technology parks, Temples of Modern and post-
modern Culture, sports infrastructure, business complexes, waterfronts, etc.),
special fiscal measures to stimulate investments in new technologies and business services, local measures to rouse labour-market flexibility (training,
incentives towards part-time and self-employment, etc.), and city marketing to
attract big international investors are considered to be the policy cocktail that
will produce new urban prosperity. Spillover effects from this capital intensive,
top-down approach to urban development are then expected to generate
employment and income in those sectors of the urban economy which are not
direct beneficiaries of the NEP.

The criticisms of this policy model are well known in academic circles (see
for example Massey *et al*. 1992 with respect to 'High Technology Fantasies').
Politically speaking this approach can be earmarked as undemocratic since it
is controlled by a small coalition of the city hall, regional authorities, and big
business. Socio-economically speaking, when applied undiluted, NEP polar-
izes urban labour-markets by promoting the growth of high skilled jobs in the
new activities and low-paid unstable jobs in the 'service annex'. Many NEP
activities also result in the extinction of existing business and trade that cannot
sustain the rise of real estate prices or the fierce competition from direct
investors. Moreover, the backward links of the new 'global' projects with the
local economies are limited, so that expenditure multipliers remain modest. In
fact many of the NEP creations respond to the logic of the global economy
favouring foot-looseness over local business confidence. In the same vein, they
also encourage inter-locality competition. In any case, despite the involvement

of the city hall in business coalitions, NEP has not generated increased control over local development potential by local authorities. Finally, NEP has also encouraged the proliferation of the dominant culture, including global consumption patterns, media symbols, and a Western bourgeois political ethos ('human rights à l'américaine').

1.3.3. Post-Keynesian redistribution policy

Orthodox views of socio-economic restructuring reject the Fordist conception of the redistribution of personal income. There is no serious concern about the loss of income for displaced workers or long-term job seekers. The belief is that in the end global free-market competition and NEP will generate sufficient opportunities for everybody.

Post-Keynesian literature has shown the latter conclusion to be false. Global competition and NEP combined do not only not provide jobs and income for everybody; they do not guarantee that low-wage workers and job seekers reach the subsistence level. Moreover, they reduce the reach of public redistribution mechanisms so that in fact NEP engenders also a lack of respect for the average human being.

According to post-Keynesian literature, redistribution policy must be continued or reinforced (Moulaert and De Cannière 1987). Even after the economic crisis of the 1970s national and personal income have continued to increase in all developed nations. But a higher share of functional income has served the acquisition and remuneration of capital, while a higher share of total personal income has gone to the technological and managerial class (high level professionals) whereas the lowest personal incomes have not increased or have suffered a loss in purchasing power. In fact in the 1980s income inequality has increased in many Western nations, especially in the USA and the United Kingdom, but also in Sweden (Gottschalk and Smeeding 1997).[1]

Given the lack of willingness of the professional and capital class to moderate its income aspirations, the basis for redistribution via social promotion in the lower job categories, and by decent minimum income guarantees through the social security or welfare system, has been eroded. Moreover, the pay of civil servants began to lag significantly in comparison with the private sector, creating a new domain of social tension and lack of professional motivation among skilled civil servants.

Post-Keynesian economics therefore advocates a reduction in working hours and a redistribution of work, new income redistribution mechanisms among socio-professional groups and between the private and the public sector, as well as the right of every citizen to a minimum income irrespective of his (or her) labour-market situation (see, for example, Cette and Taddéi 1997).

---

[1] In contrast with the USA and the United Kingdom, Sweden had a very generous social security system. Therefore, the effects of increasing inequality meant less hardship for the population than in the two other countries.

Post-Keynesian economics also explains how redistribution policy becomes more effective and finds easier funding if it is orchestrated at the international level. In the literature this is called 'international Keynesianism' and has arisen as a reaction to the neo-liberal criticism that Keynesian policy models are completely outmoded in an economy based on global competition (Moulaert and Vandenbroucke 1983).

1.3.4. Locality-rooted development policies

If post-Keynesian redistribution policy offers an alternative to NEP at a national and possibly international level it does not fill the gaps at a local level. Redistribution policy is mainly a national competence, in which local authorities and development agents can only intervene through their political lobbying and, although only at the margins, local welfare schemes. Local development strategies should follow their own agenda and respond to the needs of the most fragile segments of the local labour-markets. They should privilege the neighbourhoods and social groups that are particularly damaged by restructuring dynamics. In doing so the focus should be on the satisfaction of basic needs, the integration of different policy domains, and the promotion of proactive democratic local initiatives.

1.4. A choice for Integrated Area Development

This book takes a strong stance against local development strategies inspired by orthodox economic analysis (flexibilization of inflexible labour-markets, globalization of markets, and the role of NEP). Its intellectual foundations—although not presented in detail here—lie in institutional economics and alternative development analysis. The former are instrumental in establishing the links between economic dynamics and institutional changes (Hodgson 1988), whereas the latter leads our interest towards the socio-cultural aspects of institutional dynamics and the role of basic needs satisfaction in alternative development (Friedmann 1992).

The response of local development analysts and planners to mechanistic and instrumentalist views of planning can be best synthesized in what we present here as the Integrated Area Development model. It is a model combining different dimensions for the revitalization of human settlements in an urban environment. Detailed case studies in Western Europe show the socio-political relevance of such a model. In short, the model calls for the integration of ecological self-production, training and minimum income strategies for excluded citizens, housing and physical environment renewal as well as political participation on the basis of grass-roots mobilization, and is presented in detail in Chapters 4 and 5.

1.5. About urban governance

As we shall see in Chapter 4, the model of Integrated Area Development devotes considerable attention to social dynamics. In institutional language we could say that no local development strategy can really work if it is not socially embedded, meaning that the relations between agents, institutions, and society should become the empowering vehicle of the development agenda. But in the Integrated Area Development model we go one step further and claim that social relations are part and parcel of the development strategy, rather than simply embedding it. This is particularly visible in the central role that social innovation plays in this development approach.

To do justice to social dynamics as an integrated part of the development approach, a broad view of governance and civil society is needed. Governance can no longer be regarded as a purely administrative category or as the rational administration of a local entity. Governance should also include 'alternative mechanisms of negotiation between various groups, networks, sub-systems, potentially empowering local government' (Le Galès 1995, 1998). But governance also refers to the complexity of social relations in society. In urban society, an increasing number of cultural, socio-economic, and political identities complicate democratic policy and administration (Autès 1997). The failure of several local development strategies is due to a neglect of these dynamics (Moulaert, Farcy *et al.* 1996).

2

Globalization, Cities, and the Social Question

The ethics of globalisation—global ethics?—is perverse. It justifies increasing inequality between continents, nations and regions. And it provides the global discourse legitimating local gentrification.

T.F.P.

2.1. Introduction

For the last ten years, the term 'globalization' has been at the heart of economic and political discourse. As we saw in the previous chapter, it is cited as a major—if not the main—driving force of contemporary economic transformation. And both conservative and progressive political forces use it as an argument to support changes in socio-economic policy.

However, to build an analysis of the changes in the world economy and society, and to propose core elements of a new socio-economic policy taking 'globalization' as a major point of departure, is problematic. After a triumph lasting fewer than ten years, this view of the world economy and society, promising a better world for most nations and populations if the economy 'goes global', is being attacked from different scientific and political angles. Within social sciences, and especially economics the 'nil nove sub sole' appraisal of the globalization discourse has become increasingly strong (see, for example, Hirst and Thompson 1996). Within political science, the self-proclaimed novelty of the globalization discourse is recognized as sharing significant arguments with nineteenth-century imperial and twentieth-century geopolitical approaches to world governance (cf. Altvater 1997). And while social and political scientists have become increasingly critical of the 'globalization discourse', globalization mechanisms are more and more recognized as multipliers of social inequality and carriers of problems of the Western economy (e.g. environmental ones, including nuclear waste, exploitation of wage labour) to less developed nations and regions. Socio-economic policy based on the economic globalization thesis has become therefore increasingly under attack on two fronts.

Firstly, there is increasing doubt among scientists regarding the relevance of globalization as a novel scientific category explaining the course of society today. Secondly, the negative consequences of 'globalization' for social justice, political democracy, and ecological balance (see, for example, Douthwaite 1996) have resulted in the mobilization of civil society, social and political movements, and groups of affected citizens.

In this chapter, we make a plea in favour of a more balanced view of 'globalization'. This should allow us to distinguish between the 'old' and the 'new' in the internationalization of world society and its cities, and to assess better the impact of globalization fever on social justice, political democracy, and ecological balance. In particular, we try to determine the extent to which so-called global dynamics affect the development potential of nations, regions, and cities. We will argue that the 'globalization thesis' is above all an ideology that poisons creative policy-making, because public and private strategists have appropriated its logic to the extent that it paralyses their autonomy in local development choices and emasculates the autonomy of public and private actors who are captive to its logic.

2.2. Globalization: new terms for economic internationalization?

The internationalization of the economy is as old as international trade. But between pre-antiquity trade relationships among neighbouring city-states and the contemporary international financial circuits controlled from just a few global cities lies a long history including significant structural changes (Bookchin 1974; Jones 1990).

Debates in social science on the growing international interweaving of national economies have focused on a variety of issues. One of the oldest, which already gained momentum in the previous century and deals with imperialism and later with centre–periphery relations, shows the uneven development between nations as a consequence of prolonged colonial and post-colonial practices (for example, Amin 1970, 1973). Later on, the internationalization of the production system and the growing significance of the multinational corporation stressed the relationship between the uneven development of nations and the international strategies of MNCs (Hymer 1972). In this way, the ground was prepared for the vast literature on multinational firms, the International Division of Labour, and World Systems Theory (Wallerstein 1979).

During the last decade, the debate has focused on the relationship between the globalization of the (world) economy and its impact on the different spheres of society—not only production and trade, but also culture and consumption norms, politics and governance, which develop more and more at a world scale. The basis for this new focus is empirical and ideological (Vandenbroucke 1998). The (re)production of social and economic structures at different spatial levels occurs in the context of the globalization of socio-economic norm systems which holds a threat to the creativity of local and regional territories. Resulting conflict, resistance, and adaptation in the (re)building of social and economic structures are more evident and of more significance in particular kinds of *localities*, namely 'global cities' or cities with significant global functions.

Contemporary literature on economic globalization and cities seeks to explain why cities score high or less high in the international or global urban hierarchy. Usually, the analysis is performed in two steps. First, the features of the globalization processes are spelled out (Thrift 1994). In a second step, urban dynamics are related to these processes (Sassen 1991).

According to Shachar (1997), the emerging global economy can be characterized by the simultaneous operation of a number of processes, that, in combination, produce the transition from an international to a global economy. These processes are:

(*a*) the systematic shift of industrial production from the USA and Europe to the Newly Industrialized Countries;

(*b*) the increasing role of capital, and especially the relationships between creditors and debtors, as the driving forces of the global economy;

(*c*) the steep rise in the role of knowledge as a factor of production and as a base of management of firms and organizations, not least the international among them;

(*d*) the acceleration of the expansion of global corporations and oligopolies and the parallel process of organizational restructuring;

(*e*) the search for a new balance of power between nation-states and corporations, which shapes cross-national coalitions that are issue-oriented and brings together sectors of the state, branches of particular industries, and even certain firms, in a world-wide network.

In addition, transnational 'plural authorities' have become more powerful and have started to replace the established system of international relations based on the power and influence of nations, by regional blocs and issue-based global agreements.

Sassen (1991) uses three arguments to relate the dynamics of cities to the globalization process. First, she claims that the economic and social trajectory of each city depends heavily on the level of its integration into the global economy. Second, she argues that more cities are becoming involved in the co-ordination of processes and managerial activities. Third, she believes that the economic base and the social order of several cities are shaped by the emerging organization of the financial sector. Cities will occupy different positions in the international urban hierarchy to the extent to which they are functionally and spatially more involved with the most innovative and most globalizing economic activities, and to the degree to which they occupy

Table 2.1. *Economic and political features of the globalization process*

Shachar (1997): globalization as the simultaneous operation of a number of processes	Sassen (1991): relates the dynamics of cities to the globalization process by the use of three arguments
(a) systematic shift of industrial production production from the USA and EU to NIC	(a) the economic and social trajectory of each city depends heavily on the level of integration into global economy
(b) the increasing role of capital in shaping the world economy	(b) more cities are becoming involved in the co-ordination of processes and managerial activities
(c) the steep rise of the role of knowledge as a factor of production and as a basis of management	(c) the economic base and the social order of several cities is shaped by the emerging organisation of the financial factor
(d) acceleration of the expansion of global corporations, oligopolies, and the process of organizational restructuring	'Cities will occupy different positions in the international urban hierarchy to the extent by which they are functionally and spatially more involved with the most innovative and most globalizing economic activities, and the degree by which they occupy significant control, co-ordination and management functions in these activities'
(e) the search for a new balance of power between national states and corporations; public and private international networking-growing power of plural authorities	

significant control, co-ordination, and management functions in these activities.

2.3. Epochal changes or accelerated trends?

The summary of features of the global (or globalizing) economy and its privileged cities presented in Table 2.1 shows the fragility of the globalization thesis. Globalization is presented as an epochal change: 'it occurred never before'. But what is the nature of this change?

First, if we look more closely at the characteristics put forward by Sassen, Shachar, and others, we see mechanisms at the heart of globalization that were already at work during the Golden Sixties and even before the Second World War. It is simply that their current impact and reach are much more intense. If globalization is in the first place to be identified as geographical processes (the wider trade relationships and especially the geo-economic organization of corporations), we should recognize that it is also the outcome of a number of other structural changes connected with geographical widening. Most of these changes can be best understood in the context of the crisis of Fordism and how corporate and financial capital dealt with it (Moulaert, Swyngedouw, and Wilson 1988). In the next section, we will develop this argument further.

Second, the real (quantitative) impact of these changes is exaggerated, either because it is difficult to provide sound empirical evidence of certain trends or due to historical short-sightedness. Hirst and Thompson (1996: 2) argue, for example, that

> The present highly internationalised economy is not unprecedented: it is one of a number of distinct conjunctures or states of the international economy that have existed since an economy based on modern industrial technology began to be generalised from the 1860s. In some respects, the current international economy is less open and integrated than the regime that prevailed from 1870 to 1914 . . . As some of the extreme advocates of globalisation recognise, the world economy is far from being genuinely 'global'. Rather, trade, investment and financial flows are concentrated in the triad of Europe, Japan and North America and this dominance seems set to continue.

Third, despite the extensive literature on this topic (Featherstone, Lash, and Robertson 1995) most authors of the economic globalization thesis do not discuss the socio-cultural aspects of globalization. This omission hides one of its most far-reaching dimensions (see section 2.3.4).

Finally, most of the intellectual reconfigurations of the globalization process omit the relationship between economic and political globalization on the one hand, and the social organization of populations (class structure, ethnic and gender relationships, spatial organization of populations in the city) on the other (but see Cox *et al.* 1997, Douthwaite 1996) (see section 2.3.4).

2.3.1. From the crisis of Fordism to globalization

One of the methodological problems in analysing globalization is that the behaviour of economic agents (corporations, banks, stock exchanges, etc.) and regulatory agencies (state agencies, supra-national institutions) is placed at the heart of the analysis. Globalization is considered as the outcome of individual behaviours, codified by the rules of the market game and the gradual relaxation of state regulations (Chapter 1.2 and 1.3). The 'global economy' is increasingly recognized as a structure to which these agents are obedient— there is no escape possible from the forces of global competition—but this structure and its history are not really explained.

To do this one needs a theory that provides a historical account of the interaction between different spheres of society, that takes into account different social forces as well as their reproduction of technology and culture. To meet these criteria we need an institutional theory that integrates technological innovation into socio-political and economic dynamics, considers the endogenous nature of consumer and investor preferences, and analyses the interaction between economic and institutional processes (Hodgson 1988).

Moreover, to establish the link between global forces and local development strategies, we need a theory that connects these forces with socio-economic dynamics and agency at the local level. In earlier work (Moulaert, Swyngedouw, and Wilson 1988; Moulaert and Swyngedouw 1989; Moulaert 1996*b*) it was analytically argued and empirically illustrated how French regulation theory responds to these criteria. It links structural dynamics in capitalist society to strategy and agency at the corporate and local level (Jessop 1990). It provides the categories to apply structural and cyclical crisis analysis to the particular character of a locality (Peck and Tickell 1992).

In this chapter, we focus on the elements of French regulation theory that are useful for an understanding of the rise and decline of the Fordist regime of accumulation. Other parts of the theory will be explained in Chapter 3, in the context of local development analysis. Regulation theory emerged in the second half of the 1970s as an offshoot of Marxian analysis, a reaction to structuralist Marxism, and a synthesis of several institutional theories within a framework using a class-struggle view of the world (Aglietta 1976; Boyer 1987). One could call it a 'meta-theory': a meta-theory defines a coherent framework of theoretical premises to which different (partial) theories can be linked (Lipietz 1988; Storper and Walker 1983; Moulaert 1987). A meta-theory is not a juxtaposition of different theories—the persiflage of eclectic analysis we all seek to avoid—but 'theory as an open process' (Jessop 1989: 16) and regulation theories are 'contributions to a continuing and progressive research program' (Jessop 1989: 8).

According to the regulationist approach, a new accumulation regime and its spatial dynamics have to be theorized as a qualitative change in the organization of productive forces under capitalist relations of production. This change is a concrete response to crisis within a given regime of accumulation. Boyer (1987: 46) defines an accumulation regime as:

The ensemble of regularities that assure a general and relatively coherent progression of the accumulation process. This coherent whole allows an absorption or a temporary delay of the distortions and disequilibria that are born out of the accumulation process itself. (Authors' translation)

The principal regularities forming the economic structure of the accumulation regime are: the connection between relations and forces of production; the type of sector and market organization (market structure, modes of competition, inter-industry relations, etc.); the nature of distribution of produced value guaranteeing the reproduction of the different classes and social groups and, hence, of the mode of production; a certain composition of social demand; a certain social and spatial division of labour.

An accumulation regime is further characterized by a structured ensemble of specific institutional forms that codify and regulate the functioning of its economic structure. This ensemble consists of spatially and historically produced concrete forms of wage relations, of competition, forms of state

Regulation theory and crisis formation

Regulation theory distinguishes between four types of crisis: (i) a crisis caused by an external disturbance (climatological change, war, etc.); (ii) a cyclical crisis: a temporary disharmony between regulation and accumulation dynamics, for which a solution is found in the existing regime of accumulation; (iii) structural crisis which either finds its origin in the mode of regulation or the regime of accumulation, or in both ('the mode of development'). Only a profound restructuring of the accumulation regime can offer a solution; (iv) the crisis of the mode of production (Boyer 1986*c*: 60 ff.)

regulation, and of inclusion in the international regime. This regulatory framework, in conjunction with the economic structure of the accumulation regime, enables one to understand spatial differentiation and concrete forms of sectoral organization as well as their spatial behaviour. It also leads to an explanation of the international economic system as the systematic outcome of the interrelationships between national and supranational forms of accumulation (Lipietz 1988; Jessop 1989, 1990; Moulaert and Swyngedouw 1991). One of the most robust concepts in regulationist theory is that of 'institutional form'. This notion portrays institutions as the crossroads of structural dynamics and individual action. One could say that it combines the more orthodox view of institutions as codifying instances and the sociological view of institutions: habits, norms, routines, established practices and rules, which pattern behaviour.

The production of regional and local space is an integral part of the concrete accumulation regime. Each regime produces specific forms of spatial organization of the production process and creates and bears witness to new or renewed forms of spatial crisis formation. Cities and regions hit by economic decline, restructuring, or closing down of 'older' industries, are left with the 'old' mode of development. At the same time, old and new territories are invaded, becoming the social spaces that produce new forms of industrial, social, and technical structures and ideological images. While these are created, the previously constructed spaces undergo dramatic transformation, trying to adapt to the new requirements resulting in the creation of new socio-economic landscapes and a new territorial division of labour (cf. Massey 1984). The characteristics and dynamics of emerging modes of organization of production, forms of technological change, and social differentiation help to clarify why certain regions are abandoned and others are not, why some areas are occupied by new regimes and others are integrated in a different way. Moreover, new modes of industrial organization, communication, and exchange (of commodities, labour, and information) establish new possibilities for, and constraints on, the overcoming of spatial problems and the opening up of new spaces for production. New combinations of technological and geographical displacement arise in response to changing social, technical, and institutional conditions.[1]

Within this theoretical framework, the Fordist regime can be characterized by the elements outlined in Table 2.2. The transition from Fordism to so-called post-Fordist or flexible production systems can mainly be characterized as a crisis of regulation. The regulatory system, and especially the regulation of international commodity, raw materials, capital, and national labour-markets could not react appropriately to the challenges stemming from international competition. These resulted from changes in terms of trade, the technological revolution, and the saturation of markets in the First World, starting at the end of the 1960s with 'creeping' inflation (Moulaert and Swyngedouw 1992).

Firms able to do so invested in new technology, particularly in the new information technologies. These investments, in combination with organizational changes, allowed firms to supply new products of higher quality and to increase productivity through process innovation. The combined effect of the

Table 2.2. *Fordist regime of accumulation and mode of regulation: a characterization*

Regime of accumulation	Mode of regulation
(a) Mass production: large-scale production units technology: mechanization and automation, production lines, non-flexible fabrication tools	(a) Wage labour relation: wage compensation for productivity gains, collective bargaining, social protection, role of the state
(b) Leading sectors: automotive, electrical appliances, petrochemistry. Typical market form: monopolistic competition	(b) Competition: monopolistic competition regulated by the state and international agreements
(c) Distribution of produced value: class: productivity wages, finance capital's income social groups: importance of professional organizations and public agents public functions: focus on physical and social infrastructure, social protection	(c) Forms of state regulation: public spending for economic stability and anti-cyclical policy redistribution of income and wealth (within middle and working class) regulation of market mechanisms participation in international negotiation and regulation
(d) Structure of social demand: health, education, social protection	(d) Integration into the international regime of free trade and the monetary system of Bretton Woods (fixed exchange rates, IMF, World Bank, etc.)
(e) Social and spatial division of labour: hierarchy of regions and cities	

[1] For a more detailed analysis of the interaction of accumulation and regulation in space, see Moulaert and Swyngedouw 1991.

saturation of markets, cost reduction, and technology competition strategies of firms transformed them into market share winners but market growth killers. Throughout the 1980s labour disciplining and strict monetary policies by the national states to control inflation, nourished a deflationary spiral causing strong increases in unemployment in most developed countries.[2] In the 1990s inflation came gradually under control and reached a historically low level.

Partly as the origin of, and partly resulting from, the mechanisms governing the restructuring of Fordism, lead firms, national states, and social groups adopted political, socio-organizational, technical, and spatial strategies that today seem quite close to the so-called global strategies. There are therefore better reasons to argue that globalization refers to 'improved' corporate practice emerging from crisis experiences, than to consider it as an epochal change of the accumulation regime.

2.3.2. Globalization and new forms of corporate practice

If by the end of the 1980s we found ourselves in the middle of so-called globalization, it meant in the first place:

(a) the enhancement of global corporate structures, trade, and finance networks, enabled by spectacular transformations in information and telecommunication technology, management and organization science, and money and capital transfer;

(b) the further integration of the First World at the expense of the intensified exclusion of the Third World from the world economic stage. In fact international trade and investment flows seem to concentrate mainly on that part of the world covered by Japan, Europe, and the USA;

(c) the rationalization of locations of economic activities. This includes the clustering of R. & D., engineering, and production in privileged urban regions, the coverage of large market areas by a limited set of metropolitan providers, and the exclusion of peripheral regions from the accumulation dynamics of global capitalism;

(d) the sacrifice of significant parts of national regulation to the global competition of corporations and market-led regulation as exerted by the IMF, the World Bank, and the World Trade Organisation.

Globalization can then be interpreted as the 'best of corporate practices' at the level of the world economy. Ideologically speaking, it presents itself as a culture of excellence; socially it is a machine of discrimination and exploitation,

---

[2] The USA personifies an exception to this rule, by proliferating the 'below subsistence level minimum wage' throughout labour-markets. In this way it returned to a pre-Fordist wage–labour relation in many sectors of its economy and its wage tension has increased spectacularly in the last 20 years (*European Economy* 63 (1997), 69).

instrumental to the privileges of a happy few with a long (geographical) reach dictating the fate of the majority of firms and populations.

An individualist-behavioural featuring of globalization within the context of the internationalization debate could be that capitalists have become much more 'selective' in their use of international space. This becomes clear when one evaluates the type of activities that globalize, which spaces and populations are involved, and which types of reactions within the regulatory world are established.

2.3.3. Globalization and social forces

If one agrees with the individualist approach to globalization dynamics, economic, social, and political agents can either conform with the ideas of 'best of corporate practice(s)' and in this way contribute to the general instalment of the global economy, or step aside and become the pariahs of the global economy. In no way will the individual behaviour of economic agents alleviate or redirect globalization forces towards more social justice. This indeed would be counter-productive to the so dearly pursued environment of global competition expected to provide in the long run a minimum level of material well-being for all individuals and households willing to comply with the behavioural norms of global competition.

But the relationships between populations and globalization dynamics are far more complex than those suggested by individual global strategies. First of all, population is differentiated with respect to capital markets (class position), labour-markets and distribution of income (production relations, professional affiliation, and status), and socio-cultural integration, etc. This leads to a paradoxical reading of the social forces at the heart of globalization dynamics. On the one hand social groups can be much more vulnerable to the consequences of globalization than the individualist approach would ever suggest. But at the same time, social forces can also resist globalization and mobilize into alternative strategies for socio-economic redevelopment. This contradictory character of social forces should become clearer from section 2.4 on, when the fragmented composition of urban societies, the lack of correspondence with NEP, and the organizing over alternative strategies for urban development are analysed.

2.3.4. Globalization: a socio-cultural process

The socio-cultural dimension of globalization is already present in the discourse of the best corporate practice (section 2.3.3) and its spatial reach, in the neo-liberal message stressing the necessity to conform with the (partly overlapping) norms of market forces, deregulation, privatization, and flexibility. But the culture of globalization reaches further, drifting on the waves of Fordist marketing and spectacular 'advances' in information, communication, and multimedia technology. Again, it is not entirely clear what is typically global about this. The technology of international communication developed perhaps more rapidly because of the intensified internationalization of production and distribution systems (Cooke, Moulaert, *et al*. 1992); and the multimedia products found an expression in the post-modernist reaction to the standardized Fordist use values. In any case, the merciless hammering of the media continues, forcing multiple diversities of images referring to uniform symbols of personal progress, needs satisfaction, etc., into 'local brains'. Both at the individual and collective level, it has become very difficult to restructure one's own mind or action programme in an independent way.[3]

Nevertheless, homogenization is not the only outcome, and, contrary to what globalization theorists would have us believe, dominant culture calls for counter-cultures. Counter-cultures arise at the local and the global level. And localized counter-cultures may globalize as well. Local cultural creativity is not dead and does not blindly conform to globally set trends. This is quite clear from local artistic initiatives or exceptional views of neighbourhood development that often become the engine of local renaissance (see Chapters 4 and 5).

2.4. Globalization as the legitimization of the new politics

The impact of globalization ideology on political environments and actors is tremendous and is supported by the corporate view of the beneficial role played by globalization. This impact includes the managerial administration models that most levels of government and state institutions tend to adopt these days. The push to remain or become competitive as a country, a region, or a locality pervades circles of public government and administration. It is inspired by the failure of economic restructuring policies in the 1970s and early 1980s, where recovery was expected from the rationalization and the spin-offs of existing traditional industries, often led by state agencies or state enterprises (Brown and Burrows 1977). As awareness of the limited ability to counter the natural course of the international division of labour grew, the content of economic policies changed. The promotion of free initiative, deregulation, the creation of favourable business environments for national and international capital, etc., became the cornerstones of the New Economic Policy. Increasing reference to global competition and NEP as the only chance to find a local slot in this global world, blinded both analysis and policy debates. The failure of the restructuring of traditional industries nourished the desire of neo-liberal thinkers, economists, policy-makers, and entrepreneurs to promote trade liberalization, deregulation, and flexibilization of the production process (and therefore of labour) as the principles of the NEP. The liberal movement revived.

---

[3] Important references on globalization and socio-cultural dynamics are Featherstone *et al*. (1995) and Robertson (1992).

Liberalism and principles of liberal economic policy had dominated the Anglo-Saxon world during most of the nineteenth century, when it was also heavily attacked on the European continent, especially by the German historical school and socialist or marxian thinkers. But its influence on the European continent grew with the rise of the neo-liberal schools of Austria and Lausanne and the collapse of the German Empire. Its influence could only be countered when the failure of contained public regulation was recognized during the economic crisis of the late 1920s–early 1930s. Keynesianism and Schumpeterianism set the context for public economic policy based on public spending, socio-economic regulation, and international monetary co-ordination. But, bit by bit, and especially starting in the early 1970s, economic liberalism regained its importance because of creeping inflation, huge public budget deficits in the USA, the collapse of the Bretton Woods agreements, and the oil shocks of the 1970s–1980s. Renewed (neo)-liberal recipes were introduced: first in the international monetary sphere—the partial return to flexible exchange rates, then in industrial policy (e.g. the proliferation of free trade and free enterprise zones), next in budgetary orthodoxy, privatization, and deregulation of labour markets. This movement of neo-liberal restoration resulted in the New Economic Policy.

But the return of neo-liberal public (non)-intervention in the market mechanism also meant the restoration of individualistic analysis of public intervention. The economy is again, as a hundred years ago with the rise of the general equilibrium model, considered as a homogeneous (or 'homogenizable') action space, with its agents responding to market signals according to rational economic principles. The analysis has become somewhat more sophisticated in that rational behaviour is now expressed in terms of decision rules instead of unattainable objectives, and homogeneity refers to norms of economic behaviour and technical features of inputs. Self-adapting forces steered by behavioural rules are believed to lead in the medium or long run to equilibria in all markets. Therefore, the NEP sees the creation of an environment of global competition as setting the stage for more opportunities for all economic agents.

In reality, however, the NEP is pursued in an arena paved with unequal opportunities that are reinforced by this policy. In fact the NEP becomes easily trapped in the following structural realities:

- the disarticulated structure of the labour-market (professionally highly skilled labour vs. unskilled labour) caused by economic restructuring actions and a labour-market policy that is restricted to flexibilizing wages and labour time, and the training of workers;
- the social and ecological consequences of the abandoning of traditional industry in the developed countries, transforming physical space into economically irrelevant areas and working populations of closed-down factories into a professionally inept workforce;

• the specific problem of the distribution of income and available work. Applying liberal recipes and the NEP leads to an increase in the population of 'working poor' and a disproportionately high remuneration of the managerial class. This puts a burden on the social acceptability of the distribution of income and therefore on social stability;

• the fragility of the deregulated institutional system shown by:

   (*a*) international global competition and the crumbling or stagnation of the social protection system;

   (*b*) the decline of the social role of the state to the benefit of the entrepreneurial state (biased regulation in favour of capital, shifts in public funds from social to entrepreneurial functions (Moulaert, Swyngedouw, and Wilson 1988);

   (*c*) the entrepreneurial state at the expense of the mediating role of the state (Moulaert *et al*. 1999).

• the fragmented structure of a local production system and its relation to global competitiveness. In fact a local economy is a patchwork of very different production systems, stemming from various periods in local economic history and replying to miscellaneous needs, with a variety of efficiency norms and modes of organization (Lambooy and Moulaert 1996).

In contrast to the forecasts, the NEP has contributed to create the environment in which its outcomes are quite uneven for different social groups. And this is no less the case at the local level. Smaller local communities can sometimes be astonishingly homogeneous in the structure of their production and social systems. But this is never the case for metropolitan areas embodying the socio-economic and political fragmentation and the ecological decay that either paralyses the NEP or increasingly disrupts the society to which it applies—or both.

2.5. Globalization and local social fragmentation

As argued in section 2.2, analysts of globalization examine the inclusion and functional significance of cities in the global economy. According to this logic, they only look at metropolitan cities which are already playing an important role in the networks of the global economy (networks of top-tier privileged cities, predominantly global cities) (see critical remarks in Moulaert and Shachar 1995; and the introduction to Moulaert and Scott 1997). Moreover, even in the case of these privileged cities, they only consider behaviour and mechanisms that are functional to the global economy. As a consequence, only a small number of large cities and their global aspirations are studied. But arguments developed in the previous sections make it clear that today's local spatial forms in their physical, economic, social, cultural, and political dimensions cannot be reduced solely to the consequences of globalization dynamics. Even if we decide to look only at metropolitan cities that are well embedded in globalization dynamics, the globalization discourse is insufficient to analyse the relationships between the urban society and the globalization process.

If globalization is conceived as:

(*a*) an advanced form of organization of the corporate world heading for global competitiveness, supported by an advanced financial and know-ledge economy;

(*b*) an alternative to the failure of national restructuring strategies, with the latter based on a coalition among national capital groups, national champion industries, and national states, and the former carried by internationally competitive new manufacturing and service industries. These industries are not specific to the globalization process, but have accelerated it;

(*c*) an internationally reproduced economic culture combining Fordist marketing approaches to promote mass distribution with post-modernist ideology about customized consumption and market niches;

(*d*) national and local entrepreneurial states bidding against each other over large-scale manufacturing, service, and real estate investments;

then the organization of local space can hardly be recognized as the sole expression of globalization at the local scale, because:

• in most large (metropolitan) labour-markets the high levels of unemployment and the social inequalities which accompany them were already evident at the peak of the Fordist crisis. The identification of localities and neighbourhoods with unemployment and poverty was already possible in the 1970s or earlier, when the restructuring of the Fordist industries was not an issue (Harvey 1973);

• the high-rise Central Business Districts are mainly a creation of the corporate structure of the Fordist production system, in which finance and related activities were significantly present from the beginning (Stanback and Noyelle 1982). New clusters of business administration, financial co-ordination, and research and development are the basis of the multi-polarity of today's large urban regions, and the decline of many older CBDs.

The 'global' urban society incorporates these developments. Globalization as an economic culture, a corporate strategy and a NEP is promoting social polarization in large cities:

• the replication of commercial distribution networks in all economic sectors (from cosmetics to tie-racks to placement or interim offices) provides an atmosphere of being an economic agent within a global economic society. And the same holds for the assimilation of the norms of flexibilization, privatization, and deregulation, which are more and more apprehended as the key messages of the new bible ordaining 'old testament' values. But these norms are also a source of continuous alienation for individuals and groups who have no access to decently paid work and to the benefits of 'the global reproduction sphere'. The latter includes élite culture, the multimedia, professional education, and international travel habits, etc.;

• competition between entrepreneurial local authorities has increased the pressure on already badly hit social groups and neighbourhoods. But there are significant differences among countries and cities, depending on the mix between social and entrepreneurial policies, and corporate and financial strategies (Moulaert *et al.* 1999, introd.);

• the development of new activities in high technology and professional services along with the further rise of personal, cleaning, food provision, etc., services promotes the already existing bifurcation in the labour-market. This bifurcation was already visible with the collapse of traditional and Fordist industries, and has been reinforced by the exorbitant wage demands of certain professional categories.

Considered this way, the combination of the NEP with private corporate and household strategies reinforces the social dividing lines produced by the Fordist division of labour and its subsequent crisis. Most forms of today's poverty and social exclusion, and contemporary urban fragmentation, can be interpreted in this way (Mommaas 1996).

2.6. The urban social question and the political answer

The urban social question today is different from that of the 1960s and 1970s. Although the basic problem remains the socio-political exclusion of groups and individuals, the economic, political, and socio-cultural conditions in which the urban social question should be tackled have changed significantly. These changes do not mean that urban communities are abandoned to uncontrollable globalization forces, but that they respond to the dialectics analysed in this chapter.

These developments are summarized in Table 2.3 in the form of an evaluation of the potentials and impediments of alternative economic development approaches in urban societies today. This perspective will be helpful as a building block for the Integrated Area Development model in Chapters 4 and 5. A distinction is made between developments and forces stemming from the Fordist era, but still active today, and those that have emerged with the new socio-economic regime of flexibility and globalization.

The '+' or potentials in the second column suggest that urban society is not a passive social entity waiting to comply with the dictates of globalization and flexibilization, but is full of creative forces capable of renewing urban society

Table 2.3. *Contemporary social, economic, and political trends and their relation to the potential for local economic (re)development* (Potential=+ Curb=−)

SOCIO-ECONOMICALLY SPEAKING

Continuing Fordist trends	Potential/Curb to alternative development
growth of large corporations and internationalization	− destruction of natural environment + growth of income and wealth + internationalization of unions
increasing division of labour among sectors and professions	+ focus of social struggle − fragmentation of working class movement
union organization and restructuring by sector	− reduction of traditional union power + new models for union action and professionalization of unions
further spread of mass consumption	− compulsive consumption behaviour + emancipation of consumer movements
rise of mass media	− diffusion of compulsive consumption behaviour + information on international community—growth of 'world' consciousness
social security system for 'working' class	− exclusion of 'non' active population + protection of working class and solidarity mechanisms

Flexibilization—Globalization	Potential/Curb to alternative development
return to core activities/SME 'religion' and practice	− fragmentation of socio-economic life + opportunities for social economy and local networking
flexibilization and deregulation of labour-markets	− quality of work and life/social protection + opportunities for new start-ups in co-operative sector/new jobs in competitive sectors
increasing internationalization of international trade	− breaking the power of national unions − ecological consequences + growing pressure on unions to further internationalization
globalization and deregulation of finance sector	− loss of socio-economic control on national capital + opportunities for co-operative and solidarity banking
selective use of urban space by financial and industrial capital	− disruption of urban fabric and neighbourhoods + 'benign neglect' as an opportunity window

SOCIO-POLITICALLY SPEAKING

Continuing Fordist trends	Potential/Curb to alternative development
social security laws protecting 'core' workers	+ social protection of important segments of population − division of working class
public spending: industrial policy, economic and social infrastructure	+ strengthening of endogenous socio-economic potential − neglect of co-operative sector
consumer movements gain in influence	+ protection of consumer rights, improved quality norms − confirming 'beefsteak socialism'

Table 2.3. *cont.*
SOCIO-POLITICALLY SPEAKING

Continuing Fordist trends	Potential/Curb to alternative development
rise of social and ecological movements	+ corrigendum for development
	+ basis of social economy
destruction of physical and natural environment world-wide	− health and psychical life quality
	+ reinforcement of ecological and neighbour-hood movements

Flexibilization—Globalization	Potential/Curb to alternative development
hollowing-out of social security system for fragile segments of labour force	− loss of social protection for large groups of citizens
	+ reflection/mobilization over new notions of social citizenship
deregulation of economic environment to promote investment in new activities	−+ promotion of new capital intensive activities
large-scale urban development programmes (WTC, docklands and waterfronts, culture temples)	−+ limited opportunities for social economy
	− appropriation of private and public capital: few links with traditional segments of local economy
	+ socio-political mobilization in threatened neighbourhoods
strong (re)regulation of international migration	+ improvement of position of settled migrants
	− exploitation of labour in 'low' segments of the market

according to a local logic. The mobilization of social groups, different modes of governance within various systems of regulation, growing international links, and the establishment of networks of local movements tell us that much (see Chapter 4).

The lack of integration of large groups of population, neighbourhoods, etc., into the 'global society' challenges the urban fabric continuously. Traditional values are preserved—although often under very difficult circumstances; 'non-global' economic initiatives are promoted—which does not exclude them from international exchange and co-operation; new forms of collaboration in and outside the workplace are attempted. The heritage of the co-operative movements, reawakened as a result of the Fordist struggles (by the green movement, housing associations, peace movements, movements for the improvement of interpersonal relationships) has become extremely important for the renaissance of urban societies. Reacting to the neo-liberal 'réveil', the co-operative 'renaissance' offers substantive opportunities for alternative local development strategies.

3

A New Approach to Local Development Analysis

One of the main problems in evaluating the impact of globalization on the action space of local development strategies and policies is the choice of an appropriate methodological framework. Such a framework should respond to a number of criteria guaranteeing both analytical relevance and an easy transition to the formulation of local development policies and strategies.

In this chapter, we deliberately choose regulation theory as the privileged analytical structure through which to organize the analysis of local dynamics. In Chapter 2, we presented regulation theory as a tool to analyse the crisis of Fordism and the rise of post-Fordism, and to reveal the relativity of the globalization thesis. From this analysis we may retain the impression that regulation theory is mainly a macro/meso theory. This is, however, a misconception: regulation theory deals with social and institutional forms and, as such, gains in relevance as it is applied to concrete social formations, regional and urban armatures. In fact, as we will argue, regulation theory is exceptionally well suited to deal with the institutional complexity of localities facing severe restructuring problems. For this reason, it is also a theory that is particularly useful for analysing the governance dynamics of a locality.

3.1. Disintegration of localities and the call for local renaissance

Since the industrial revolution, Western Europe has sacrificed a significant part of its natural environment and social cohesion to economic growth and the elimination of mass poverty. The establishment of heavy industry since the end of the eighteenth century, the massive industrialization which lasted until the *inter bellum*, the spread of Fordist industries (automobile and petrochemical industries, domestic electrical appliances), and the Fordist mode of consumption lifted the material well-being of most of the population to historically unprecedented levels. But these developments were extremely costly in terms of the attendant impact on natural resources, the environment, and human communities.

When, towards the end of the Fordist regime of accumulation, traditional pre-Fordist industries (mining, steel, shipyards, textiles, etc.) as well as many

branch plants and production facilities of the Fordist production system
started closing down, the consequences of the devastation became visible,
especially in regions with traditional industry (Moulaert, Swyngedouw, and
Wilson 1988). Numerous living communities continued to exist at the fringes
of industrial derelict land, as their housing stocks deteriorated and the general
health of the population declined, unemployment continued to grow, and only
the most dynamic groups were able to leave their settlements for a more prosperous destination. In the heyday of neo-liberal restructuring policy, impoverished populations in 'fragile' neighbourhoods became, in political terms, a
quantité négligeable. A main outcome of the shift from Fordist to 'post-
Fordist' social policy was the marginalization or the 'disintegration' of entire
neighbourhoods and communities from 'mainstream' society.

Aspects of the decline and restructuring of localities have been examined
extensively. Since the beginning of the crisis of Fordism in the 1970s, different
approaches have developed, which can be classified according to: (*a*) the
methodological perspective; (*b*) the spatial level concerned; (*c*) the economic
structure of the area; (*d*) the view of local redevelopment that is adopted by the
researchers. The literature can be divided in five main study categories that
succeed each other more or less in time:

• The economic restructuring of old industrial regions
• The locality studies
• Industrial districts and flexible specialization
• Disintegrated localities
• Sustainable development at the local level.

The first approach—economic restructuring of old industrial regions—
which is, historically speaking, also the oldest, concentrated on the study of the
decline of old industrial regions, and was not innovative with respect to redevelopment or restructuring policies. Some studies were still quite optimistic
about the future of traditional industrial regions. They believed that appropriate restructuring of existing industries combined with industrial diversification
could save the economic prospect of regions whose economic history had been
written by coal mines, steel plants, shipyards, etc. This logic can, for example,
be found in the debates within RETI (the association Régions Européennes de
Tradition Industrielle) in the 1980s. Gradually the shortcomings of the traditional restructuring recipes in these regions and their main cities became visible
and a new approach, the locality studies, gained momentum. The focus of their
detailed analysis was the decline and its consequences, for the economic,
social, and political conditions of the local population (Cooke *et al.* 1992;
Harloe, Pickvance, and Urry 1990). But the locality studies missed a policy
perspective. Doom thinking, or a shift in analytical focus from losing to potentially winning regions and to flexible production systems, emerged as escape
strategies from the ailing Fordist restructuring recipes, calling for increased

productivity, process innovation, and specialization within existing industries. For about ten years the industrial district model was propagated as the example for local development and socio-economic renaissance (Brusco 1982, 1986). But the growing conviction that this model was of a limited and geographically confined applicability (Amin and Robbins 1992; Martinelli and Schoenberger 1992) led scientific interest towards other theorization of economic regions and firms. 'Losing or disintegrated localities', and the need to design specific strategies for them, became important topics. This renewed interest in old industrial cities, or specific neighbourhoods of large urban regions, was also reinforced by the massive ecological and social problems which these areas face, and by the growing fear among dominant social groups that decaying neighbourhoods could become the ultimate executioners of the capitalist system.

3.2. Regulationist theory: its role in local development analysis and strategy

3.2.1. Accumulation and regulation at the local level

As we saw in Chapter 2, the production of regional and local space is an integral part of the concrete accumulation regime. Each regime produces specific forms of spatial organization of the production process and creates and bears witness to new or renewed forms of spatial crisis formation. Cities and regions hit by economic decline, restructuring, or the closing down of 'older' industries, are left with the 'old' mode of development. At the same time, old and new territories are invaded, becoming the social spaces producing new forms of industrial, social, and technical structures, as well as ideological images promoting this reproduction. While these are created, the previously constructed spaces undergo dramatic transformation, trying to adapt to the new requirements. As a result new socio-economic landscapes and new territorial divisions of labour are created (cf. Massey 1984). The dynamics of emerging modes of organization of production, forms of technological change, and social differentiation can help to clarify why certain regions are abandoned and others are not, why some areas are occupied by new regimes and others are integrated in a different way. Moreover, new modes of industrial organization, communication, and exchange (of commodities, labour, and information) provide new possibilities for, and constraints on, the overcoming of spatial problems and the opening up of new spaces for production. New combinations of technological and geographical displacement arise in response to changing social, technical, and institutional conditions.[1]

---

[1] For a more detailed analysis of the interaction of accumulation and regulation in space, see Moulaert and Swyngedouw 1991.

Regulation theory has adopted a number of biases echoing the shortcomings which we usually attribute to orthodox economic analysis. Because of their particular meaning to the application of regulation theory for local development analysis, we should discuss these *biases* in detail.

An exaggerated or even exclusive reference to economic rationality as a driving force for individual and collective economic behaviour, with a subsequent neglect of non-economic rationality and irrationality, and of non-economic spheres of social reality

Economic rationality in the sense of the *homo economicus* reduces economic behaviour to the calculated pursuit of an economic optimality objective (utility, profit, income, revenue) under the hypothesis of full information. As rational behaviour is considered to be one of the structuring principles of society—the average behavioural rule reflects the main features of behaviour within a structure *or* of structural determination—it is only a small step from economic rationality to 'economism'. Godelier (1972) defines 'economism' as 'the reduction of all social structures to nothing but epiphenomena of the economy which itself is reduced through technique, to a function of adaptation to the environment' (p. xxxiv).

It would be an unacceptable exaggeration to say that regulation theory stands for economic rationalism and economism. The theory studies in the first place social structures and regulation in economic subsystems of society. It therefore mainly focuses on economic behaviour and how it relates to different spheres of socio-economic life. But this socio-economic focus does not justify the often observed technicist reading of production systems. By this we mean, for example, reducing a mode of development to a technological paradigm (for a critique, see Leborgne and Lipietz 1990; Cooke, Moulaert, *et al.* 1992), thus sharpening the profile of the behaviour of the entrepreneur as 'technologically based, economically rational'. This, in turn, reinforces the limitation of the analysis of production and entrepreneurial models to those adopting the dominant behaviour of flexible specialization, and in high technology and professional services production ('flex spec prof high tech'). Analysis thus excludes other production models in agriculture, services, handicraft, etc., either situated in the 'informal sector' or at the boundary between the formal and the informal economy (cf. Hadjimichalis and Vaiou 1990). This logically unnecessary narrowing of focus could harm the applicability of regulation theory to local development where informality is often a key issue.

But the scent of economism in regulation theory reaches farther and affects the notion of regulation itself. Radical geographers like Hadjimichalis and Vaiou (1990) and Leontidou (1990) rightly draw attention to the regulation of informal activities. In the mainstream regulationist literature, however, regulation is seen as instrumental to the development of the new dominant production model. Some scholars correctly argue that regulation is too often interpreted as 'economic regulation' and 'we therefore need to move the debate out of the realm of economic imperatives which have tended to dominate discussions on regulation' (Marden 1990: 1).

A functionalist view of forms of regulation characterizing a regime of
accumulation and, therefore, a lack of interest in social reproduction outside
the economic and political sphere

It is indeed a small step from 'economism' to economic functionalism, or even to political economic functionalism. Marden (1990) and Jessop (1990) warn against the tendency of these (regulationist) approaches towards functionalism.

'Functionalism' is understood here as the deterministic impact of one logic of existence on all spheres of being. In addition, this logic is 'rationalized' (like the logic of 'the rational economic man') and leaves little room for determinism and behaviours that are antagonistic to the main rational logic. One cannot accuse the founders of regulation theory of having built a functionalist trap into their basic framework of analysis. However, by stressing the production system with its economically rational behaviour, as well as the regulatory behaviour piloting or guiding it, one opens the door to functional determinism. Certainly, regulation theory distinguishes between social relations corresponding to different structures of society as well as their functional complementarity. But by emphasizing the pervasive nature of the dominant economic behaviour, there is a danger that the economic rationale is not only considered as explanatory in the last instance, but is also believed to affect the relative autonomy of behaviour which is guided by socio-cultural, political, and other rationales as well. When that happens, cultural and political differentiation cannot be used as an explanatory factor for differences in development patterns between areas. For example, the lack of recognition of relatively autonomous socio-cultural dynamics in any such impoverished application of regulation theory conflicts with findings on the differences in urban development patterns between core and peripheral nations and regions. Leontidou (1990: 256–7), for example, observes that '. . . certain aspects of cultures around urban questions can be contrasted effectively, and to a great extent explain contrasts in urban development patterns between core and peripheral societies'.

The lack of analytical status for non-economic dynamics also reduces the significance of different types of social struggle in historical development (Markusen 1983). History then becomes economically determined, and class struggle is narrowly read as capital–labour conflicts over income distribution. Spontaneous movements on issues in the political, and especially the socio-cultural and ecological reproduction sphere, are considered as historical accidents or predictable by-products of what is going on in the socio-economic sphere. Power relations are given a mainly economic reading and social reproduction in the consumption sphere is primarily interpreted as an extension of what is going on in the production sphere. These observations point to the heart of the explanation as to why regulationist analysis until now has devoted little attention to social reproduction dynamics in urban settings under post-Fordism (Wolch and Law 1989).

The combination of a flavour of economism with functional determinism leads to an even narrower understanding of the mode of regulation. There is a strong tendency in the literature to confine social regulation to socio-*economic* regulation by state authorities, in the light of the achievement of a leading economic development model (see again Marden 1990). The step from functional determinism and economic dominant behaviour to technocratic voluntarist policy ('political economic determinism') as the dominant form of regulation is indeed small. Regulation becomes functional agency: state regulatory agents guide economic behaviour into the 'correct channels'. This is perhaps the strongest bias in the application of the regulation framework in socio-economic geography. Many scholars regard regulation as confined to state regulation. And for some among them, this regulation is meant to guide the diffusion of the dominant production model. Observe, however, that this reductionism is in conflict with the original definition given by Boyer (1986*c*). For Boyer,

the mode of regulation is the ensemble of procedures and behaviours, individual as well as collective, with the triple feature of: (i) reproducing the fundamental social relationships through the conjunction of historically determined social forms; (ii) supporting and piloting the accumulation regime; (iii) assuring the dynamic compatibility of a large set of decentralised decisions, without the necessary internalising of the principles of economic adjustment of the whole system by the actors. (1986*c*: 54–5)

Unfortunately, little work has been done by the founding scholars of the regulation school on forms of regulation other than state regulation and collective bargaining. This is probably due to the original focus of the analysis on macro-economies, where other forms of regulation such as habit formation and behavioural codes, cultural patterns, etc., were assumed to play a less important part. However, at the level of local and regional production systems, a more social reading of regulation dynamics, in all its dimensions, is an absolute necessity. In this respect, we follow Hadjimichalis and Vaiou when they argue that a close examination of the relationship between formal and informal activities might be quite instructive for understanding the diversity of regulatory forms:

Attention needs to be drawn on how institutionalised and informal systems of social control and diverse social factors interrelate with the process of uneven development. (1990: 90)

Such an examination might be instructive for a more socially complete discourse on the accumulation and regulation dynamics of historically determined local and regional economies. Historical analysis shows how informal regulation based on norms and reciprocities becomes more important in societies (or fragments thereof) where 'formal' regulation fails. From the point of view of the regulation school, periods of transition from one mode of regulation to another would therefore show an increased presence of informal 'regulation'. The reform or replacement of Fordist regulation both in core and peripheral regions proceeded in parallel with illegal employment in many sectors, subcontracting to 'informally' organized firms, or, to use a more tangible image, the rise of textile and footwear sweatshops. And in many European countries, this informal regulation preceded the loosening up of labour and social security regulations (Moulaert, Leontidou, *et al.* 1993).

A 'missing link' of articulation between modes of production and between regimes of accumulation, leading to a neglect of production systems other than the dominant one when analysing a regime of accumulation

Simplified application of the regulationist framework leads to representation of the national economy as a macro-outcome of the interaction between contemporary flexible accumulation and a regulatory system in which flexible organization and regulation gradually take over from the Fordist mode of regulation. In this way, an economy is displayed in which modern technologies, new activities, flexible modes of work organization, deregulation, etc., represent the state of economic art. But reality is much richer. Systems of production typical of previous regimes of accumulation continue to exist. And regulatory dynamics are a combination of historical forms of socialization and contemporary innovations in social regulation. Economies are a patchwork of traditional and new activities, of culture and manufacturing, of small-scale agriculture and mass education, of flexible organization and rigid professional codes, of guilds rooted in the Middle Ages and professional old-boys networks from the 1970s. In large cities, this patchwork is visible in the physical forms of various connected or disconnected neighbourhoods: modern and post-modern administrative complexes, remodelled nineteenth-century factories housing SMEs, traditional historical centres renovated according to neo-gothic and classicist design with traditional personal and retail services or liberal professions, run-down working-class housing built in the nineteenth and twentieth centuries, indecipherable webs of transportation and communication routes.

A lack of balanced dialectics between different spatial levels and spatial forms in socio-economic systems

This is maybe the most unfair of outsiders' criticisms of regulationist working methods. Most research based on the theory of regulation deals with macro-economic and sectoral case studies, and takes supranational or national contexts into account—often more than any other theory dealing with problems of economic reorganization (Moulaert and Swyngedouw 1992). There is, however, a deep-seated prejudice against regulation theory. Its critics claim that it is a macro-economic theory and that, therefore, when applied at the local level, it lacks the categories that would permit both a proper analysis at that level and an examination of the links with other spatial levels. However, the analytical categories used by regulation theory are social and institutional in nature, and as this chapter will show can be used at all levels of space and aggregation.

An uncritical pluralism of micro-theories that are used to 'fill' the regulationist framework, leading to a strong presence of orthodox concepts and theories, stemming from conservative currents in institutional and evolutionary economics, and business economics, but also borrowed from dominant economic and socio-political practice

When looking at the local level of analysis only, one notices that restructuring dynamics as analysed from a so-called regulation point of view are explained by use of neo-institutional or neo-classical industrial economic categories in which rationality, mechanistic learning processes, etc., are dominant features. As such, the 'econonism' of some regulationists is expressed in the uncritical selection of economist partial theories (e.g. transaction cost theory to explain networking behaviour). Terminology stemming from neo-institutional readings of market mechanisms and economic co-operation (Cooke 1988), from labour contract theory on social struggle (e.g. wage-bargaining; Boyer and Orléan 1990), and from public administration approaches to the state (Goodwin, Duncan, and Halford 1993) unfortunately exerts an increasing influence on regulationist thinking.

A neglect of ecological dynamics

Some regulationists recognize the devastating effects of capitalist accumulation on the environment (Lipietz 1992*a*, 1992*b*; Altvater 1993) and ascribe a special role to environmental movements in social change and for ecological targets in progressive policies. Nevertheless ecological concerns do not yet belong to the core of the regulationist research agenda.

3.2.2. Reformulating regulationism for local analysis and strategy

A more socially complete discourse of spatial development should avoid the biases illuminated above. This can be accomplished by establishing a better balance between structural dynamics and historical specificity. This balance can be pursued by recognition of the relative autonomy of different structural dynamics in society, whose interaction gives rise to different regulatory dynamics following mixed rationales. This also implies that concrete institutional forms can only be identified for historically concrete social formations, regions, and localities. In addition, the concepts of social conflict and power relationships must be rehabilitated and the discourse of the dominant economic model replaced by one considering the articulation between modes of production and regimes of accumulation in historically concrete spatial structures. It might then very well make sense to talk about 'local production systems' and 'local modes of social regulation', embedded in higher order spatial systems (Peck and Tickell 1991; Goodwin, Duncan, and Halford 1993).

An articulate reading of economic development in a spatial structure through different modes of production and regimes of accumulation includes particular forms of coexistence between new production models, in their different forms, and 'older' production models. Such a reading will permit a distinction between forms of organization and regulation of production systems with different technological, socio-economic, socio-political, and socio-cultural features. The history of local and regional forms of accumulation and regulation is built on the articulation between the current and previous modes of production and regimes of accumulation (Lipietz 1977); present layers of accumulation and divisions of labour depend on previous ones. Uneven development can only be well understood by looking at the dialectics between 'new' and 'old' forms of accumulation and regulation or between different layers of development (Massey 1984: 117–18).

The process of uneven development is significantly determined by social struggle and power relationships among social classes and groups at different spatial scales, and regarding different issues (Markusen 1983; Massey 1984). For the regulation approach to be capable of incorporating power relationships into regulatory dynamics, it has to recognize different kinds of struggle. This requires a good understanding of the interactive dynamics of structural rationality (economic and political, for example) in functionally determined institutions. Social dynamics of the economic structures go far beyond accumulation and market dynamics, or the organization of work. They also include power struggles: economic control has a political dimension. And this dimension is far more vigorous than suggested by the institutional labels of the settings in which 'the economic' takes place. The discussion on the 'network firm', for example, cannot be conducted exclusively in terms of economic functionality (e.g. complementary assets provided by different partners); it needs to deal with the control network of firms over firms, capitals over capitals, interest groups over interest groups, internal as well as external institutional frameworks in which the different partners in the network operate. For regulationists the debate concerns not only what is 'between markets and hierarchy, i.e. alliances', but also: (i) hierarchy in markets and alliances; (ii) markets in hierarchies and alliances. In other words, power relationships are recognized both in markets and network organizations; and economic transactions reinforce the control mechanisms within 'non'-market organizations (e.g. generalization of profit & loss responsibility, of transfer pricing within firms). The analysis of the forms of regulation stemming from new forms of economic 'co-operation' is based on the dialectics between production, exchange, and control, and cannot solely be made in terms of the legal institutional aspects of that co-operation (Leborgne and Lipietz 1990; Krifa and Moulaert 1991). A priori, 'horizontal' forms of organization of production and distribution follow the same logic of uneven spatial development as the hierarchical model of the large firm including its forward and backward linkages does. In fact, by increasing possibilities of organizing economic activities over a global scale, this new 'economic co-operation' might even reinforce spatial unevenness.

Restoring the balance between structural dynamics and historical specificity in regulationist socio-economic geography requires the identification of concrete institutional forms belonging to historically concrete social formations, regions, and localities. This historical articulation of spatial development could ward off the danger of a general model whose key elements are believed to explain transition in the majority of localities and to a comparable extent (Thrift 1989).

These conceptual and methodological inputs into the analysis of spatial development can be summarized in seven points:

(i) The articulation between subsequent modes of development and their different concrete forms must be integrated into the analysis. All layers of the socio-economic development of the regions and local communities under investigation must be considered, not in a chain model involving subsequent stages, but as historically articulated elements of a contemporary socio-economic structure.

(ii) The impact of non-economic structural dynamics on regional and local economic development must receive more attention. Regional and local development is to a large extent locally bound and dependent on socio-cultural and political dynamics. From the perspective of economic development, one must realize that economic targets and policy instruments may vary strongly among types of territorial economic structure. In many regions and localities, not high technology and business services, but personal services, small-scale and artisan manufacturing, specialized agriculture, agro-tourism, or cultural activities are more likely to become the prime engines of redevelopment.

(iii) The concept of regulatory dynamics must be broadened from 'pure economic regulation' and 'state agency' to different types of formal and informal regulation. In addition to the roles of political authorities and government agencies as makers of laws, regulations, and administrative rules, and as implementing as well as controlling agents, there is the whole world of formal and informal codification of social behaviour. Habit formation, behavioural rules, control practices, the building of constraints, and opportunities for individual and collective actions are also part of the world of regulation. There may be formal organizations behind these institutional dynamics (groups based on kinship, employee organizations, churches, etc.). But institutions can equally emerge from the spontaneous interaction between individuals or groups of individuals affected by similar recurrent, dramatic, events or circumstances.

(iv) The role of agency and behavioural codes must be redefined in correspondence with the broader definition of institutional dynamics. The consequences of this redefinition for the study of regional and local development are significant. First of all, the role of agents, individual or collective, cannot be structurally forecast. It is analysed within the context of 'structural and behavioural contingencies' characterizing the tensions between social forces and social structures in a region or a locality at a certain period in history (Jessop 1989; Low 1994). This leaves a significant role for behaviour other than that which is structurally or institutionally envisaged, as well as for the proactive role of agents in changing institutions and structures (cf. Giddens, in Cassel 1993). Second, the role of the state in regional and local development can only be fully understood if the overall institutional complexity of the state is taken into account. This means that the state is not only the state of political and financial administration, of collective bargaining, the one in charge of running the welfare system and playing the role of the rational planner, but that it is also the object and the arena of strategies and struggles in many spheres and institutions of society. From this point of view, the state is not only a fragmented state, responding to numerous social forces, but has also developed dynamics of its own, which in certain regions and localities make it completely unfit to lead any development policy whatsoever (Moulaert and Willekens 1984).

(v) Social reproduction at the local and regional level requires extensive study. In line with the previous recommendations, social reproduction in all spheres should be analysed. It cannot be reduced to either the reproduction of skills and attitudes of the workers on the shop floor, or the development of the consumption norm in the sense of changes in the composition of the basket of goods and services consumed by households (Moulaert and Swyngedouw 1989). Instead, the focus must be on the reproduction of humans in all their individual and social existential dimensions, i.e. as agents in their local communities with a physical, biological, and socio-cultural level of existence.

(vi) There must be an integration of different spatial scales. A more correct application of regulation theory not only implies articulation among subsequent modes of economic development, but also between different spatial scales (Swyngedouw 1992). Neither accumulation nor regulation can be spatially isolated. That they adopt specific territorial forms is evident; but these forms are produced in the midst of a local–global interplay, all at the economic, political, and socio-cultural level. Therefore, when interrogating these forms, we must scrupulously investigate the links between the different spatial scales of structural dynamics and of agency affecting territorial development. Local components of accumulation and regulation must be recognized; different spaces of regulation within a nation exist (Goodwin, Duncan, and Halford 1993). But structural coherence at the local level cannot be grasped or challenged without taking into account its interaction with the regional armatures and social formations in which it is embedded or with which it interrelates (Lipietz 1977).

(vii) Power relationships, both social and political struggles, are critical analytical categories in regulation theory. Power relationships cannot be appropriately studied without taking into account class relationships and struggles, economic monopolization of capital and other factors of production, as well as political domination based on economic control and non-democratic decision-making procedures.[2] To deal with relationships of power and struggle in an adequate way, regulation theory must fully elucidate the consequences of a world full of conflict, dominated by an economic structure dependent on the outcome of the struggle between capital and labour. Economic, social, political, and other domains are entangled at all spatial levels and their struggles are played out within the world's institutions. Thus power relationships must be included in the analysis of different types of institutions and their regulatory dynamics at the local level. This should be the case in the socio-economic domain (Swyngedouw 1989, 1992), in the political domain (Jessop 1990), and in the socio-cultural domain (Harvey 1989; Eade 1997).

Regulation or governance?

There is some similarity between the critical reconsideration of the notions of regulation and regulatory dynamics on the one hand, and that of governance on the other hand. The notion of regulation has been criticized for its connotation with state regulation, with economic functionalism (policies instrumental to rational economic goals), and its reduction of institutional dynamics to formal regulation. We argued earlier that a revisited notion of regulation must take these criticisms into account if it is to be useful for empirical investigation. The notion of governance has undergone a comparable reconceptualization. Apart from the insights of institutional economics regarding the forms of regulation of the economy already discussed, political science and sociology have contributed to this endeavour. Borrowing the term from international and national policy networks studies, political scientists have applied the concept of (local) governance in the analysis of those changes in the social and economic sphere that have affected local government: economic globalization, political and institutional changes, and demographic trends. These changes have resulted in a crisis in legitimacy and efficiency of local government. In response to this crisis, new structures and procedures of service provision, mainly special purpose bodies, public–private partnerships or private and voluntary agencies, have emerged; local governance refers then to the system of regulation and co-ordination governing the interaction among such a plurality of actors. Governance includes formal but also informal, non-governmental mechanisms, based on the reciprocal recognition of interdependence and on the shared goals of the actors involved. More recently, in the work of political scientists as well, the concept of governance has begun to encompass

---

[2] Because of their approach to the social world, labour contract theory and neo-institutional approaches to the regulation of economic life can only deal with soft forms of conflict between economic agents or socio-economic groups; they offer neither an analytical, nor a political solution to overt disequilibria in power relations and struggle.

different types of regulation, not only political, but also economic and social, active within a specific territory (Le Galès 1998), so that the previously clear-cut demarcation between government—state or local—-market, and civic society has become blurred and needs to be redefined. Sociologists have developed a similar concept when discussing local forms of regulation. Following Polanyi, economic sociologists in particular were interested in showing how much the market was embedded in the local society, particularly in areas such as the Third Italy where the functioning of the market is deeply dependent on community institutions, family structures, and local subcultures (Bagnasco and Trigiglia 1993). Local regulation is then a process which involves different types of regulation, reciprocally adjusting to each other. All these scholars stress the importance of some local resource to direct the interaction among different actors towards co-operation. Some scholars point to *trust*, both among individuals involved and in the institutions, as the base on which interorganizational co-operation is built (Bagnasco 1994). Some speak of *social capital* as a set of characteristics of society such as trust, norms of reciprocity, and networks of civil associations, which facilitate co-ordination of individual actions (Putnam 1993), others of *institutional thickness,* a quality of a specific locality which, again, nourishes relations of trust and innovative capacity (Amin and Thrift 1995). Whatever the terminology used, the focus is on specific forms of social relations among institutions and individuals, which are supposed to be conducive to socio-economic development. In this definition the notion of local governance and that of local regulation tends to coincide and we will use these terms interchangeably. It is in this definition that the concept of governance supports our view of the centrality of social innovation as a crucial factor in strategies of local (re)development.

(viii) The integration of the dialectics between nature and society (ecological processes and planning) also plays a part. Nature is to be considered as the most primary resource of social progress and should be preserved and reproduced according to this status. Regulation theory is primarily concerned with social relations of development, an issue that is sometimes overlooked in the 'ecological development literature'. The relationship between sustainable development and regulation theory is quite instructive in this regard.

Regulation theory and sustainable development

Are sustainable development and regulationist approaches competitive approaches? Should regulationism replace sustainable development as a theoretical device of local society, because the former in contrast with the latter is capable of dealing with the complex social relations in the city? Or, conversely, should the sustainable development approach replace the complex regulationist approach, which does not privilege the ecological dimensions of local society?

The view which we defend here is that it is preferable to integrate both approaches, but that regulationism as a meta-theory is better fitted to host the key categories of the sustainable development approach than the other way around.

There is no doubt about the need to combine economic restructuring with sustainability issues in local development analysis and practice. Until today, in economic restructuring literature, even from a regulationist perspective, the 'environment has been marginal to the [economic] restructuring research agenda' (Gibbs 1996: 1). But the opportunities to combine economic restructuring and ecological development concerns offered by regulation theory are promising.

(*a*) Although not innovative in this respect, regulationist analysis has shown how the capitalist mode of production has devastating ecological consequences. The few existing contributions (Lipietz 1992*a*, 1992*b*; Altvater 1993) show the exploitation of the natural resources but also that 'The re-edifice of social relations—where people relate to one another with money and commodities on the market—causes natural constraints on production and consumption to disappear from the consciousness of society. Nature only becomes relevant when it imposes additional costs or disrupts human life' (Altvater 1993, cited by Gibbs 1996: 5).

(*b*) Regulationist analysis shows the complexity of the social and political relationships accompanying economic restructuring. It therefore offers a unique framework to anticipate the institutional dynamics stemming from a combination of ecological and economic restructuring strategies. It shows quite clearly that market-led regulation will not be adequate to resolve the current environmental crisis. It also argues that the 'economic–ecological impasse cannot be simply treated as an ethical problem with the solution in changes of behaviour' (Gibbs 1996: 6), but that special institutions equipped with administrative and sanctioning competencies must be called to life.

(*c*) Regulationist analysis at the local level theorizes the absence of generally applicable development itineraries (see previous sections). It argues that it is certainly 'out of the world' to predict that decentralized, small-scale production systems would be ecologically gentler (Gibbs 1996). It is most improbable that without appropriate institutional dynamics and socio-political struggle, local production systems and public authorities will pursue ecological targets.

(*d*) Simply adding ecological targets to the list of strategic objectives cannot guarantee the integration of environmental concerns into local development agendas. It needs a confrontation between economic, social, and environmental goals, and an integration of the social dynamics supporting or opposing ecological concerns into the local development process. This is certainly the case at the level of the city which, because of its immense reliance on land and other natural resources, manifests itself as an intrinsically unsustained system, with little flexibility to restore the resources it uses. 'Planning for sustainability' at the local level means planning as a social process (Matthews 1996: 44). It also implies a multidimensional sustainable development agenda, with 'five "goals" . . . in the fields of *resource conservation, built environment, environmental quality, social equity* and *political participation*' (Matthews 1996: 36).

But 'planning as a social process' does not only mean the involvement of all concerned interest groups in the planning process. This would be an optimistic view of community dynamics, built on the conviction that contradictions can be overhauled and that social engineering will ultimately produce a compromise planning agenda. For it may very well be that the local community development agenda is in strong conflict with dominant economic forces or that the consciousness of community identity is insufficient to support a local development strategy. These contradictions are best analysed by use of regulation theory.

3.3. A regulationist interpretation of local disintegration

Regulation theory provides an analytical framework for the study of the development, decline and re-emergence of localities. In particular, 'winning' regions and localities, or regions and localities with promising restructuring perspectives, have been the object of analysis (for a survey, see Moulaert and Swyngedouw 1989, 1991). Our own work is more systematic in responding to the criticisms discussed in the previous sections. Economic decline, exclusion mechanisms, redevelopment strategies, and regulatory dynamics have been studied in twenty nine localities within the countries of the European Union (Moulaert *et al.* 1992, 1993, 1994a, 1994b; Moulaert and Leontidou 1995).[3] In the sections that follow, we use the main results of these studies to illustrate what we understand by a regulationist analysis of local development in so-called disintegrated localities. In Chapter 4, we employ the same theoretical framework to analyse alternative development strategies and their regulatory dynamics. Chapter 5 examines in greater detail development dynamics, strategies, and institutions in four metropolitan (Antwerp, Bilbao, Hamburg, Rostock) and two 'sub' metropolitan areas (Charleroi as a part of the traditional Walloon manufacturing basin; and Girona as part of the hinterland of Barcelona).

3.3.1. Analysing local development

To respond to the criteria discussed in the previous sections, the analytical framework should provide guidelines to identify the following key elements:

(i) The specific forms and history of the production system(s) in a particular social space;

(ii) the concrete institutional forms that the mode of development adopts in a historically defined region or locality;

---

[3] The names of the localities can be found in Table 3.5.

(iii) the social forces and the collective or individual actors that have influenced the development of the area;

(iv) the local regulation or governance system.

When regulation theory is refined as explained in the previous sections, it should accomplish the following analytical assignments:

• The identification of *the overall structure of a society* taking into account the balances and imbalances between social forces and structure, competition and co-operation between classes and groups, in a complex constellation of local, regional, and national communities, with different sub-subsystems showing complex grids of interaction.

• *The categorizing of different subsystems constituting the socio-economic structure of the locality* including forces at work at 'higher' spatial levels (regional/national, supranational) but with significant interaction with the local level. These subsystems characterize different elements of the local economic, social, and political structure. Table 3.1 provides a list of the different elements in each subsystem at various spatial levels and suggests potential links between them to be explored in empirical analysis. It also lays the groundwork for identifying the different forms of regulation and governance at play in the dynamics of these subsystems.

Labour-markets, for example, are considered according to the specific features of their spatial scale. Local labour-markets are only exceptionally really 'local'. Most of the time, they are embedded in a broader spatial dynamic, either because firms and their demand for labour operate on a regional, national, or supranational spatial scale; or because local labour supply is reinforced or weakened by commuting or migrating workers. Moreover, state regulation and labour bargaining are usually national or regional processes, in which the local plays a self-adapting role. It is probably only in locally based production systems, training and education patterns, self-employment, and informal labour practices that the 'local' is relatively autonomous. This autonomy will increase, as the local comparative advantage (culture, research and development potential, good practice in co-operative relationships, etc.) becomes stronger.

• The identification of regulatory dynamics at the local level with a distinction made between economic and non-economic regulation, state and non-state regulation, informal and formal socialization in the system of governance. This assumes that regulation is defined in a non-functionalist, non-economist way, and comprises the socialization processes and their outcomes that codify or direct individual and collective behaviour and attitudes in the local subsystems. From this point of view, the classically used model of instrumental regulation or administrative governance, which infers one or a few agents and politically determined laws and rules established by state bureaucracy, is only a special case of regulation. The long list of regulatory forms in Table 3.3 is meant to illustrate the complexity of regulatory dynam-

Table 3.1. *Subsystems of a local community and their different spatial levels of existence*

Subsystem	Spatial scale		
	Local	Regional/national	Supranational

Production system
  labour process
  technology
  sectoral/market
  structure
	Small/medium-sized
	  enterprises
	Branch plant
	Independent worker
	Family business
	Production/trade/
	  technology networks
		National/regional
		  enterprise?
		Technology
		  transfer?
		Regional/national
		  market?
		Intermediate trade
		  flows
			Transnational
			  corporation
			Intra-firm trade
			Alliances
			Subcontractor
			  networks

Labour-market
  skills
  jobs
  labour time
	Local labour-market
	  mechanisms
	    formal and
	    informal
	    self-employment
	    self-sufficiency
		Integration in larger
		  regional market
		  division of
		  labour
		  migration
		  commuting
			Integration in firm's
			  international division
			  of labour
			International migration

Reproduction of
  labour
    households and
    education
	Household economy
	  structure and skills
	  gender relationships
	Local school system
		Migration and
		  commuting
		  household
		  members (workers,
		  students, . . .)
		Transfer of income
			Migration and
			  commuting household
			  members (workers,
			  students, . . .)
			Transfer of income

Reproduction of
  labour
    housing and
    living
    environment
	Housing stock
	Renovation processes
	Social quality of
	  neighbourhood
		Imitation and
		  learning effects
		Development of
		  regional lifestyle
		  profiles
			Internationalization
			  and homogenization
			  of life and living
			  styles

Political agencies
  and institutions
	Local authorities and
	  administrations
		Regional/national
		  authorities and
		  administrations
			Supranational
			  authorities and
			  administrations

Planning agencies and strategies	Private/public/mix	Private/public/mix	Private/public/mix

Issue-oriented
  movements
    political
    ecological
	Mobilization on local
	  or global issues
		Same regional issues
		Regional
		  mobilization on
		  local issues
			Same international
			  issues
			International
			  mobilization on
			  issues of regions,
			  localities

ics, not to reproduce them exhaustively. Two steps are required to arrive at this table. First, we reproduce a table from Peck and Tickell (1992) (Table 3.2 in the present chapter), which illustrates how economic regulation occurs at different spatial levels and provides room for the definition of non-economic and informal forms of regulation and their interplay.

The stress which Table 3.2 places on economic regulation probably explains why in Peck and Tickell's approach civil society and households remain somewhat undeveloped as domains for regulatory dynamics. This is a pity, for it is often there that a discourse on informality and non-economic regulation begins: the household and the embedding family as the ultimate environments for relations governed by reciprocity; the civil society as the prime scene for associative relations in spontaneous issue-oriented initiatives. Another problem with Table 3.2 is that it insufficiently reflects inequality in power among the agents involved in regulatory dynamics. Regulation is often the outcome of dominance of one group over the other; the regulatory behaviour (law and norm setting, penalization and incentives, imposing dominant codes for informal socialization) in different subsystems of society reflects uneven access to power and resources. Countervailing movements often 'go informal' because formal socialization structures are completely 'congested' by tradi

Table 3.2. *Economic regulatory forms at different spatial levels*

Regulatory form/ mechanisms	Spatial scale		
	Regional/local	Nation-state	Supranational
Business relations (inc. forms of competition)	Local growth Coalitions Localized inter-firm Networks	State policies on competition and monopoly Business representatives bodies and lobbying groups	Trading frameworks Transnational joint venturing and strategic alliances
Labour relations (inc. wage form)	Local labour-market structures and institutions Institutionalization of labour process	Collective bargaining institutions State labour-market and training policy	International labour and social conventions Regulation of migrant flows
Money and finance	Regional housing markets Venture capital and credit institutions	Fiscal structure Management of money supply	Supranational financial systems Structure of global money markets
State forms	Form and structure of local state Local economic policies	Macro-economic policy orientation Degree of centralization/ decentralization in state structures	Supranational state institutions International trading blocks
Civil society (inc. politics and culture)	Local trade union/ production politics	Consumption norms	Globalization of cultural forms
Grass-roots governance	'Gendered' household structures	Party politics	Global political forms

Source: Peck and Tickell 1992.

tional socio-economic and political institutions, or by traditional value systems. Therefore, grass-roots movements (about such issues as the environment, housing, gender, etc.), informal and alternative economic initiatives, and new political parties, often constitute the most creative forces for socio-economic restructuring at the local level.

In Table 3.3, an attempt was made to include these informal and power relationships in the regulatory dynamics of local society. The term 'informal activity' remains somewhat ambiguous, however: it may mean escaping state regulation; or it may mean slipping outwith market regulation; or it can mean both. Other classifications of informal activities are possible (Mingione 1991: 8); some of them are quite relevant in the discussion of particular subsystems in concrete localities. Power relationships are articulated with different subsystems and types of regulation in the table. They represent domination by one type of agent over others; or they are countervailing powers, resistance, and change movements. A priori, without empirical verification, it cannot be forecast whether informal regulation or economic regulation would incorporate more oppression than formal or non-economic governance respectively. Formal subcontracting relationships, i.e. those confirmed by a formal agreement between principal and subcontractor, can be more exploitative for the subcontractor than reciprocally agreed subcontracting relationships in the black economy; and cultural discrimination can be more alienating than the payment of subsistence wage levels for ethnic minorities. In the same vein, gender, ecology, or culture-oriented community grass-roots movements can become more effective in managing the capitalist wage–labour relationship than corporatist unions, etc. (see e.g. Fisher and Kling (eds.) 1993).

• Regulation theory is used as an analytical structure, based on a meta-theoretical framework (Jessop 1989, 1990; Moulaert 1987). The research agenda must be adapted on empirical grounds. If we examine regions/localities in decline, we should study those subsystems, regulatory dynamics, and partial theories that are helpful to understanding the specificity of such areas. Customizing the regulationist approach for regions and localities in decline leads to the identification of different types of problem areas and to theoretical explanations of decline that are seldom found in textbooks on regional development but cluster more or less around such types (see section 3.3.3).

Table 3.3. *Types of informal and formal regulation of local societies*

Subsystem/ institution	Type of regulation			
	Economic regulation		Non-economic regulation	
	Formal	Informal	Formal	Informal
Product/factor markets	Quality normalization Competition laws (state) Business opening times (local state)	Reciprocal subcontracting relationships	Health and safety protection rules	Cultural exchange among managers operating in markets
Sector organization	Technology propriety rights Anti-trust laws (state)	Informal networking re. technology, management Informal subcontracting among firms	Pollution control regulations (regional or local state)	Political lobbying at different spatial levels
Organization work process/ labour exchange	Labour laws Labour market institutions Job hierarchies	Partial black wage labour Employment without contract Non-registered domestic work	Regulation of work circumstances (state/region)	Informal socio-cultural associations of workers
Household economy	School laws Official educational programmes Marriage laws	Domestic child employment Gender division of labour	Legal protection of minors Protection of rights of partners	Religious and cultural habits Organization of leisure time
Housing	Housing market Mortgage market Zoning regulations (local)	Shared occupancy Illegal occupancy Informal building activities	Health and safety regulations and control	Tenant organization on legalization, renovation issues
Educational system	Laws, programmes Administration of educational system	Parent associations for fund-raising (the friends of . . .)	Organization of retraining and promotion of teachers	Club activities: organization of socio-cultural events, etc.
Political institutions	The entire body of state economic regulation (all spatial levels)	Informal lobbying on economic issues	Voting system Organization of municipal authorities, etc.	Informal lobbying on non-economic issues
Planning agencies	State and market agencies for local economic development	Grass-roots initiatives for local economic development	Establishment of legal forms promoting local emancipation	Mobilization on non/or not exclusively economic issues
Issue movements Grass-roots governance	Intervening in various forms of regulation. Examples: bargaining over work conditions, ecological regulations, local investment policy, gender relationships, etc.			

Source: Moulaert 1996a.

3.3.2. The study of socio-economically disintegrated areas: specific analytical requirements

When, as in this research, 'socio-economically disintegrated areas' are the focus of the analysis, even more analytical precautions must be taken. In fact most theories belonging to different disciplines in social science clarifying growth and prosperity, well-being and governance in regions and localities, usually offer only limited possibilities to explain economic decline, socio-economic disintegration, and social exclusion. The explanation of bad fortune cannot simply be stated in terms of the anti-symmetrical mapping of the mechanisms generating fortune and prosperity.

In our work, a 'socio-economically disintegrated area' has been defined as an area partly or entirely cut off from the major economic development processes, and from the 'winning' areas which were significantly, and with positive socio-economic results, involved in one or more of these processes (Moulaert *et al.* 1990; Moulaert, Leontidou, *et al.* 1992; Moulaert and Leontidou 1995). Localities can be said to be disintegrated in at least three ways. First, there is the sense of disconnection from the general processes of prosperity in the neighbouring or larger spaces that encompass them. Secondly, the mechanisms that nourished or should have continued to nourish economic growth may have come to a stop. And thirdly, localities can be disintegrated in the sense of fragmentation and segmentation among different groups of the local society. If social segmentation can be considered a basic feature of a competitive society, spatial disintegration forces due to economic failure reinforce it.

The following questions arise from an analysis of socio-economically disintegrated areas. What are the mechanisms divorcing a locality from the processes of prosperity and well-being? What are the specific factors in each subsystem reinforcing decline? Which particular assets are available to foster redevelopment actions? In Table 3.4 mechanisms of disintegration and processes of re-emergence are related to different subsystems.

One can perceive an asymmetrical character *vis-à-vis* what happens in the case of virtuous development processes in most subsystems of a local community. Not only do the positive mechanisms which are analysed in growth and development-based theories disappear, stagnate, or invert, but other mechanisms based on parallel initiatives, destruction, escapee behaviour, disillusion at the collective and individual level, etc. develop as well. Let us look at theories concerning two subsystems shown in Table 3.4: the production system and the reproduction of labour system. Theories of local development based on high technology strategies and theories of industrial and technology districts all point out how success can and has been reached, but not how decline could occur or how the need for alternative redevelopment strategies may emerge (Bingham and Mier 1993; Moulaert and Delvainquière 1994). The latter are covered by theories of decline and socio-economic disintegration and redevelopment stressing 'parallel' or

Table 3.4. *Mechanisms of socio-economic disintegration at the local level and processes of re-emergence*

Subsystem	Production system	Labour-market	Reproduction of labour: households and education	Reproduction of labour: housing and living environment	Political agencies and institutions	Planning agencies and strategies	Issue movements: social, political, ecological
Production system	Decline of leading sectors Drop in investment	Job redundancies No job creation	Possible closure of schools Decline in educational level	General decline of urban environment	Loss of political impact/image	Loss of effectiveness New planning priorities	Establishment of parallel production circuits
Labour-market	Loss of dynamism in labour supply	Rising unemployment Mismatch S/D	Low motivation of students Orientation problems	Loss of income housing, education Motivation problems	Pressure for replacement income and jobs	Job creation priorities New planning priorities	Movements aiming at job creation Alternative work circuits
Reproduction of labour: households and education	Distrust *vis-à-vis* employment possibilities in salaried labour relations	Bifurcation in labour-market strategies: multi-jobs, training, liberal professions or independent labour	Intra-family tensions, migration . . . Lack of motivation Decline in standard of living		Pressure on youth and education policy	Call for training programmes; on the job training	
Reproduction of labour: housing and living environment	Declining investment environment	Declining labour-market environment . . .		Segmentation in living environments for families	Demand for social housing Demand for security policy	Demand for improvement of social housing programmes	Housing movements, squatting
Political agencies and institutions	Sectoral policy: restructuring versus innovation	etc.	etc.				
Planning agencies and strategies							
Issue movements: social, political, ecological							

'informal' development dynamics (Moulaert 1996*a*). With respect to the reproduction of the labour system, conflicting views clearly arise between liberal social
mobility and human capital theories on the one hand, and community development models on the other (Storper and Walker 1983). If the first type of model
stresses the significant positive correlation between education, training, and professional advancement, the second clearly underscores the reproduction process
in the broad sense in which local communities play a notable role, either positively or negatively. The building of a labour relationship, or even the existence
of work opportunities, depends to a large extent on the socio-cultural and socio-
economic well-being of the community where potential or employed workers
live.

A socio-economically disintegrated area is susceptible to mechanisms of
social-economic disintegration which, even if their relevance is generally
accepted, may vary significantly among localities. Moreover, neither the
mechanisms of disintegration, nor those of redevelopment can be theorized by
use of the optimistic categories of small and flexible production systems. The
theoretical explanations needed to understand decline and redevelopment
potential in the different subsystems of the localities are at least partly different from the theories capable of elucidating local stories of growth and prosperity (Moulaert 1996*a*). To give only a few examples: micro-theories of the
flexible organization of high technology and advanced producer services in
successful regions must be replaced by theories of unequal sectoral development and the socio-economic disintegration of the locality. And theories of
efficient allocation of labour in local labour-markets will be overruled by theories of labour-market segmentation and disequilibrium. Theories stressing
inertia and local governance will be preferred to theories of political decision-
making. If these 'parallel' or 'alternative' theories often radiate absolute pessimism, they are needed to understand the mechanisms of decline in local
societies. For without this realistic understanding of the downward spiral of
the local community, no positive action for strategy and policy directed at
renaissance is possible.

Redevelopment in a disintegrated area as compared to a 'winning' or prosperous area involves particular challenges. In a successful area, redevelopment
strategies are based on trust referring back to previous successes; in a disintegrated locality, for lack of successful experiences, trust needs to be replaced by
hope. But hope is not a powerful motivation; therefore, scarce human and economic resources need to be mobilized at their full strength.

3.3.3. A typology of localities—first general results

In our empirical research, we observed the existence of at least six socio-
economic types of localities in decline: (i) rural communities; (ii) semi-rural
communities with miscellaneous light industry; (iii) semi-rural communities
with metal and textile industries; (iv) urbanized coal-mining communities; (v)

urbanized communities with a metallurgical tradition; (vi) harbours. Each of these types has a different history of sectoral economic development and decline. At the same time, they each raise questions about various facets of the socio-economic structure such as the organization of the local production system, the natural environment, the informal organization of labour processes, the institutionalized and non-institutionalized labour movements, the housing and land markets, politics and political administration, socio-cultural relationships, local governance, etc.

Table 3.5. *Economic structure of localities*

Type of community				
Rural communities	Semi-rural communities with miscellaneous light industry	Semi-rural communities with metal and textile	1. Coal mining communities 2. Metallurgy communities 3. Harbours	Special cases
Spatha (GR) Almeida (PT)	Maniago (IT) Vigevano (IT) Montes de Oca (SP) Arganil (PT) Ostiglia (IT)	Urbania (IT) Roanne (FR) Castres-Mazamet (FR) Agueda (PT)	1. Rhondda (GB) Valenciennes (FR) Charleroi (BE) Dortmund (DU) 2. Lavrion (GR) Elgoibar (SP) Bilbao-Barakaldo (SP) Charleroi (BE) 3. S. Cardiff (GB) Calais (FR) Bremen (DU) Hamburg (DU) Antwerp (BE) Rostock (DE)	Fishguard (GB) Sykies (GR) Aveiro (Beira Mar) (PT) Perama (GR) Gerona (SP)

Source: Moulaert, Leontidou, Delladetsima, *et al.* 1994*a*.

The Appendix lists the variables that are potentially relevant for studying the restructuring crisis of localities in decline. For the purpose of this book, the restructuring crisis of the localities can be summarized by use of a limited number of variables: (*a*) the degree of diversification in the sectoral structure; (*b*) the urban versus rural character; (*c*) the cohesion of the local production system; (*d*) the level of responsiveness of the planning agents and the local institutions to restructuring problems. The first two variables correspond to a more socio-economic development-based reading of local dynamics. The last two variables belong to the local regulatory dynamics or governance. They require a sociological and political reading of local dynamics. It is especially for the analysis of the three last variables that regulation theory has shown its value.

The first variable, i.e. the sectoral structure (the nature of the dominant sectors, the degree of diversification) obviously explains a large part of the seriousness of the crisis, its consequences, and the possibilities of the locality to overcome it (see Moulaert and Leontidou 1995). But for at least half of the localities analysed (the smaller traditional manufacturing cities, most of the rural communities with a miscellaneous sectoral structure, and some special cases—see Table 3.4), the three other variables also play a significant explanatory role.

Let us illustrate this for the second variable, i.e. the urban versus rural character of a locality and for the fourth, i.e. the responsiveness of local development agents.[4]

Urban versus rural character

The intensity of the crisis and its repercussions on different subsystems and social groups in the localities is strongly influenced by this contrast. Rural and semi-rural localities that in general are also smaller localities—in our sample their population ranges from five thousand to a hundred thousand inhabitants—have a stronger absorption capacity for unemployment than larger urban areas. This is due to the family structure and the role of the informal economy in the locality. Besides the most rural localities (Almeida, Spatha), where the boundaries between the 'family households' and the agricultural sector firms are often hard to draw, smaller semi-rural cities with restructuring problems in manufacturing (Urbania, Comarca Montes de Oca) have sought relief in informal employment. These cities experienced shifts to informal employment as a natural ingredient of restructuring when 'formal' employment opportunities became scarce.

Shifts from formal to informal employment or combinations of formal with informal jobs not only represent a flexible mode of organization of production and work processes, they also help resolve low income situations. In urban economies with a long history of traditional manufacturing sectors, the model of the large family has declined among people who have lived in (semi-)urban settings for a long period, possibly for many generations. However, the possibility of disguised unemployment and informal employment in large family structures remains quite relevant for families of migrants originating from communities where informal labour and large families are pillars of societal dynamics. Interesting cases have been observed not only in the south of Europe (Sykies, Perama, Elgoibar) but also in the more northern Roanne.

In the northern urban areas we studied (Antwerp, Hamburg, Bremen, Valenciennes, Charleroi), the absorption capacity of the economy when faced with unemployment is relatively small. Therefore, the need for more formal decision-making and formal strategies to create new jobs is perhaps stronger

---

[4] For the third variable, the cohesion of the local production system, we refer the reader to Moulaert *et al.* 1994*a*: ch. 2.

here than in semi-rural or rural localities, or in larger urban localities in southern countries. It is remarkable to observe that not only differences in business culture and the presence of the rural family reproduction model, but also the sectoral structure of the locality affect the sense of informality in work relationships. Throughout Europe, textile manufacture seems to rely more on informal work situations than the steel and metal transformation industries. The fragmentation of the textile production system into innumerable units, its similarity with working traditions in agriculture, and the high level of 'homeworkers' and of the hidden employment in the sector help to explain the relationship between informal work and textile production (see Martinelli 1988).

The gravity of economic crises is also catalysed through the structure of the housing market and its diverse character in rural and semi-rural localities compared with strongly urban localities. Housing problems may be experienced in completely different ways. The same objective housing quality can be perceived as bad or as good/acceptable housing. The informal use and self-construction of housing can provide relief for people who have housing quality problems. Only one rural locality (Spatha) was found to have housing problems, while all urban localities going through economic restructuring also exhibited significant housing quality problems.

In addition to the urban–rural contrast, the nature of informality differs among the various countries, and especially perhaps between northern and southern countries, because of differences in laws and regulations as well as in enforcement practices. For example, formal control of illegal and informal practices is much stricter in Antwerp than it is in the Thessaloniki area. The mushrooming of illegal textile workshops is possible in the latter, but less so in Antwerp. In the same way, the social relations typical of the large family in rural environments are encountered in a much weaker form in the northern urban centres than in the southern urban centres. This may to a certain extent be a matter of proximity to the dominant production organization model. But it is also a matter of regulation and formal control by state authorities and of concessions by the state to the family unit (the 'household') to compensate for deficits in personal incomes, provision of social services, and housing, that is, reproduction costs in general.

It was found that the role played by informal work and production systems in localities is ambiguous. On the one hand, they function as buffers to unemployment and absolute loss of income, they often contribute to local social cohesion, and, in labour-intensive activities such as clothing and footwear, they consolidate the competitive position of local production systems. On the other hand, they often impede organizational and technological innovation as well as social progress. In this way, even if they contribute to the cohesion of the local community in the short run, in the medium run they *may* prevent economic innovation and therefore accelerate the process of local socio-economic disintegration.

Responsiveness of local development agents

The fourth variable affecting the impact of the restructuring crisis, with consequences on the localities, is the responsiveness of planning agents and local institutional systems to the crisis mechanisms, and the dynamism of the networks in which grass-roots movements and the public and private economic agents are involved. These are of course important elements of the local regulation or governance system.

For many but not all localities, there is a close connection between the cohesion of the local production system and local responsiveness (Moulaert *et al.* 1994: ch. 2). In fact, localities with a disintegrated production system seem to have very poor powers of social and political mobilization regarding the design and implementation of local development strategies.

Localities with similar spatial and functional cohesiveness in their production system may nevertheless possess different development potential. Therefore, development potential seems to be further influenced by other variables. We will discuss four additional variables: the public institutional system, the quality of the local authorities, the collaboration between different public and private agents, and the involvement of the European Union. The latter will be discussed in Chapter 5.

The public institutional system

In general, localities that can rely on a strong intermediate or regional authority as a kind of countervailing power, or as a leverage, to stimulate national state action, are better off than localities which cannot rely on such an authority. From comparison of the case studies, it appears that a strong regional system within a national quasi-federate or confederate state system has, in principle, a positive influence on local economic development (Moulaert *et al.* 1994a: ch. 3). In such a system, intermediate levels such as regions act as immediate partners in networks that can support regional and local economic development, and in which public as well as private agents can play a part. A major concern arises, however, when intermediate state levels assume the role of an ersatz central state and, like the latter, interfere with the competencies and the financial autonomy of the local level. This could be because major administrative reforms have left existing local competencies unadjusted to changes in the relationships between the central and the intermediate levels. Moreover, the lack of clarity in competencies or the transitional character of certain intermediate structures can seriously affect the activities of the local state.

'Quality' of local authorities

Even in strong regional systems, where a substantial part of decision-making power has been delegated to the regional and local level, the local authorities are sometimes of poor quality. This quality concerns the technical and professional capacities of the political and administrative personnel, including the planning agents and technicians assisting them. But it also concerns political balance and co-operation, political equilibrium or disequilibrium within the municipalities or municipal districts. As for technical and professional capacities, these are quite uneven across localities. They have been summarized in Table 3.6, following the same categories of localities presented in Table 3.5. Integrated planning approaches are treated as a special resource. They will be a key topic in Chapters 4 and 5.

Virtually none of the localities holds all of the types of resources necessary to lead a coherent development strategy. Most of the largest industrial cities and ports combine all types of skills; but Bremen, Dortmund, and (South) Cardiff do not use an integrated planning approach. Among the smaller traditional coal and metal manufacturing cities none has a uniformly positive 'skills

Table 3.6. *Economic structure of localities and the resources of local authorities* (+ = available resources; − = non-existent or of poor quality; no mention means no particular problem; ? = unclear situation)

Type of resources	Type of locality				
	Rural communities	Semi-rural communities with miscellaneous light industry	Semi-rural communities with metal and textile	1. Coal-mining communities 2. Metallurgy communities 3. Harbours	Special cases
Organizational capacity	Spatha−	Maniago− Vigevano+	Roanne+ Castres− Mazamet+/− Agueda− Urbania+	Rhondda− Dortmund+ Hamburg+ NE Antwerp+ Valenciennes−	Gerona+ Sykies+ Beira- Mar+/−

Technical skills		Arganil+
		Comarca
		  Montes de
		  Oca−
		Ostiglia+
			Agueda−	Charleroi+
				Elgoibar+/−
				Barakaldo−
				Valenciennes+
				NE Antwerp+
					Fishguard+
					Perama−
					Beira-
					  Mar+/−

Financial resources	Spatha−			Rostock−	Perama−

Planning perspective: integrated approach	Spatha−
	Almeida−
		Vigevano+/−
		Ostiglia+/−
		Comarca
		  Montes de
		  Oca+
			Urbania+
			Castres−
			Mazamet+/−
			Agueda+
				Bremen−
				Rhondda+/−
				Charleroi+
				Dortmund−
				S. Cardiff+/−
				Lavrion+
				Elgoibar+
				Calais−
				Hamburg+
				NE Antwerp+
				Valenciennes−
				Rostock+/−
					Fishguard+/−
					Sykies+/−
					Beira-Mar+/−
					Perama+
					Gerona+

agenda'. Localities of the semi-rural type with miscellaneous light industry or metal and textile industry that score relatively well on the skills scale are Vigevano, Urbania, and Mazamet. Note that quite a number of localities utilize integrated planning perspectives, but lack some of the skills to put them into practice: Comarca Montes de Oca, Agueda, Lavrion, Elgoibar, Perama. An outlying locality that scores well for all skills and planning criteria is Gerona.

As far as the political balance is concerned, no detailed analysis has been made in this research. Obviously, the preparation of glamorous integrated development plans has a political aspect. 'Grand plans' are often meant for electoral purposes or to hide disagreements between political parties ruling the communities. In certain localities, municipal councils simply consist of smaller parties blocking each other. In such a case, very little effective decision-making is occurring and very few new initiatives for local economic development can be launched. But the case studies show a number of very interesting examples for collaboration between different spatial levels in the political system. In certain cases, inter-government co-operation helps to overcome political stalemates at the local level.

Public–private collaboration

Most localities have made efforts to set up such collaboration: their development is more or less coalition driven. However, some localities have virtually no collaborations between the private and public sector: Rothopos, Beira-Mar. While some localities exhibit problems in building or rebuilding such partnerships: Agueda, Castres-Mazamet, Lavrion, Elgoibar, and Rhondda. Large cities, especially ports, do quite well in public–private networking, but tend to prolong their economic activity in traditional sectors (Hamburg). Innovative private–public networking forms have been observed in Antwerp, Bremen, and Dortmund. As to the smaller localities, new forms of public–private networking emerge in Almeida, Arganil, Gerona, and Urbania.

3.4. The link between analysis and strategy

Local development strategies are part of the development history of a locality. To understand the role of strategy and policy in development, it is essential to study the development trajectory. In other words, to use the fashionable and useful term launched by Paul David in innovation economics: development and development strategies are path dependent (David 1975; Moulaert *et al.* 1999). And in the tradition of institutional economics in general, in particular regulationist theory, the development trajectory includes the history of institutional dynamics, and of local regulation and governance. It is not possible to understand and assess local development strategies without having made sense of the history of the institutions in which they were embedded in the past.

In the next chapter we argue in favour of an integrated area development approach as an alternative to economist functionalist top-down approaches to development planning. The latter orthodox view is confronted with a basic needs approach to local development. The satisfaction of basic needs is one of the pillars of integrated area development. The other is innovation in the social relations of development. Together they constitute the 'social innovation' view of territorial development—as opposed to the technical view of innovation in orthodox regional innovation.

4

Integrated Area Development and Social Innovation

In advanced capitalist societies, especially over the last couple of decades, people on average are investing less in family, relationship and community capital and more in human, corporate and market forms of capital. This is an important instance of a shift from social to private forms of capital, which is similar in some ways conceptually to the shift from ecological to business capital . . . This trend is troublesome because it reduces the social safety nets that people can depend upon during stressful socio-economic times, and reduces the quality of life for the most vulnerable.

(O'Hara 1997: 6)

4.1. Introduction

Relative and absolute poverty are increasing considerably. This is the result of a lack of social aid for unemployed labour, the exclusion of the long-term unemployed from social compensations, the depreciation of the status of the unemployed to that of 'poor' (a transition from the social security sector of unemployment to the welfare sector), and the shrinkage in the lowest wages that has led to a growth in the number of the 'working poor'. Moreover, 'liberated' economic mechanisms have generated an unacceptable distortion between the purchasing power of disfavoured groups of the population on the one hand, and the cost of housing and the use values of the information society (information networks and technology, quality education and culture, etc.) on the other. An increasing number of the poor are driven towards homelessness and exclusion from the assets of the information society, which today are considered critical for finding access to decent jobs and for professional mobility.

Like slow-working hyper-poisons, the neo-conservative or neo-liberal recipes for curing the economic crisis have affected the logic of Western society and politics. Within business circles, large-scale private economic initiatives, instrumental to global competition are considered to be the main forces for economic revival and the reintegration of excluded citizens in society. An analysis of neo-liberal social cynicism and its recipes for economic revival was offered in Chapter 2. The challenge in the present chapter is (i) to show how the orthodox view of socio-economic development does not worry about the role of excluded people in economy and society; (ii) to present and defend an alternative philosophy for economic development; (iii) to explain the Integrated Local Development model; (iv) to think about the role of social movements within the social relations of local development.

The second section compares traditional economic development with alternative development approaches (Friedmann 1992; Ekins 1992; Mayer 1995; and Moulaert *et al.* 1996), while the third section presents the Integrated Area Development model as a synthesis of alternative local development. This synthesis focuses upon social relations and their role in the genesis of social innovation in local development strategies. Social innovation is first of all concerned with the modes of integration of objectives typical of the social economy within a coherent action framework. Among these are quality shelter, professional training, job opportunities, urban renewal, small firm start-up, and neighbourhood governance. In the fourth section, the specific role of social movements within local governance and innovation strategies is examined.

4.2. The logic of alternative local development

4.2.1. The failure of mainstream development approaches

The difficulty in providing an accurate normative and descriptive definition of development is not a new problem, but the aggravation of socio-economic inequalities has lent renewed urgency to this issue (European Commission, Eurostat, Statistics in focus).

Within the 'rich countries', the increase of produced wealth has continued, although the growth rate slowed in the 1970s as a consequence of transformations in the production system and the social organization on various spatial scales after the oil price shock of 1973–4. However, the new urban poverty has reignited the debate on the relations between the well-being of social groups, economic growth, and the social security and welfare systems (Benassi, Kazepov, and Mingione 1997).

Starting in the 1960s, the confrontation of rich and poor countries provoked a stream of ideas and thematic movements searching for an alternative or a 'real' mode of development, setting the improvement of living and working conditions for all citizens as a prime goal. Alternative development was first discussed with respect to Third World countries (Hammarskjöld Foundation 1975; Palme Commission, ICDSI 1982; Brandt Commission 1983; Brundtland Commission, WCED 1987), and is based upon the principles of more fair trade, curbing the arms race, and sustainable development. But the challenges of 'alternative development' increasingly affect so-called 'developed' countries and indeed the entire world population. Economic and social evolution, as well as the problems of democracy in the developed countries themselves, can be questioned from the viewpoint of the philosophy of development. Several initiatives should be cited. The Cocoyoc Declaration (1974) draws special attention to the satisfaction of basic needs and respect for the earth's natural resources. 'Counter-development' based on new social values and institutions allowing for a richer valorization of already acquired knowledge, instead of new technological developments, is mentioned by Jakob Von Uexkull in the preface to Paul Ekins's book (1992) on the new world order and the role of social movements in global change.

4.2.2. The orthodox development approach

According to the orthodox view, development is assimilated to the pursuit of capital accumulation and the 'creative destruction' of existing production units to promote economic growth. This viewpoint does not reflect the innovative role of the Schumpetarian entrepreneur, but a narrow deterministic and technologist curtailment of it.[1]

The indicators of development used in the orthodox approach logically avoid questions about the social and geographical distribution of production and income growth, and ignore their negative 'external' effects. Production activities causing the destruction of the natural and social environment, or which are meant to soften, correct, or prevent the negative impact of economic development, are accounted not as costs but as sources of growth and progress. Ecological and social questions are avoided. The more time you spend in traffic jams, the more fuel you consume, the higher GNP will be. And the larger the number of the socially excluded, the more significant will be the growth in GNP of social services, even if those services only partially meet the needs of the people concerned; and therefore, again, GNP increases.

According to the orthodox approach, inequality is a constitutive element of the nature of development (see again Chapter 2). Limited redistribution is the answer to guarantee minimum consumption levels and welfare services for the least favoured segments of the population. Moreover, such services can become a flourishing sector of the economy. This is obviously a dangerous view of combating poverty, taking the fate of less fortunate people as a market-creating factor, with markets that are profitable thanks to the misery of the clients.

4.2.3. Alternative development

The alternative approach is based upon the idea that development should in the first place satisfy the basic needs of the most marginal groups of population. These are needs for decent accommodation, medical care, education,

---

[1] For a confrontation of different views of innovation according to Schumpeter, see, for example, Gallouj 1994.

local democracy, etc. Their alienation reflects the delicate or 'indecent' side of the development of a nation, a region, a city, or a community of people. In fact the condition of the most marginal among its citizens is a key criterion when evaluating a community.

This approach to development integrates qualitative criteria. The one-sided approach to inequality that is strictly oriented to minimum consumption levels is seriously questioned: the recognition of a broader conception of the needs, functions, and rights of individuals and groups should result in a renewal of actions against poverty.

This broader conception does not limit the possibilities of development, but helps to focus on the living and working conditions of fragile socio-economic groups. If in purely human terms this seems self-evident, it implies a real rupture with the orthodox approach to development. In fact, within a broader conception of living and working conditions, individuals are recognized as agents seeking autonomy or self-determination in the construction of their existence. The rejection of individual submission to constraints over which, according to the orthodox development view, no control is possible, and the explicit choice of alternative development to overturn these constraints, are first priorities. John Friedmann (1992) considers this consciousness-raising as an important dimension of 'empowerment' (auto-activation).

Normative elements for alternative development

This approach to development, based upon the satisfaction of basic needs, implies a change in the nature of action by, and in favour of, the least-favoured segments of a population. The consumption level is not the only criterion to judge their situation; access to the means enabling the satisfaction of basic needs is equally pertinent. At the same time, local development becomes less a question of guaranteeing purchasing power, and more one of promoting a structural change to improve the individual and collective potential to respond to needs, and thus to participate in a production process aimed at the satisfaction of the basic needs of all.

From this viewpoint, the individual household should play an active and productive role, no longer exclusively that of a passive consumer. This active role can be achieved as a result of productive action and of the rediscovered capacity of individuals to respond to their basic needs. Excluded citizens become the instigators of the solution to their own problems. This dimension conforms to the general aim of empowerment: individual participation and self-determination through alternative development. Friedmann (1992: 33) maintains:

As its central process, an alternative development of households and their individual members in all three senses [social, political, psychological] . . . Alternative development must be seen as a process that seeks the empowerment of households and their individual members through their involvement in socially and politically relevant actions.

Note that the individual productive role which is an essential ingredient of the alternative development approach, cannot be interpreted as a tribute to the market, but rather as the recognition of the human potential to resolve its own economic difficulties. This principle does not exclude that of solidarity with non-productive people. Moreover, without collective organization it cannot be applied.

Alternative development is based on the satisfaction of basic needs, economic and social mobilization, and the political dynamics allowing the establishment of enabling institutions.

Several authors have stressed the natural links between these dimensions. First of all, there is the intrinsically social character of basic needs themselves: not only the need for a basic income, material resources, and shelter, but also for expression, creativity, conviviality, and self-determination. This multidimensionality of basic needs is cited by all authors on alternative development referenced up to this point. Second, following Friedmann (1992: 31f.), we should underline the relationship between the social and the political movement: no social empowerment without political empowerment. According to Friedmann, alternative development implies not only the improvement of material conditions but also, and above all, political empowerment. The focus is on needs and rights, and not on desires and interests. Third, there is the centrality of social relations among development actors. Moulaert and Delvainquière (1994) use the concept of social innovation in local development terms. In the same vein as Ekins (1992), they sustain the importance of innovation in social relations, more than any other form of innovation. According to these authors, it is only by developing new forms of revealing needs, of cooperation, and of democratic management, that the basic needs of the most deprived citizens will be recognized and met. If, at the conceptual level, the role of social movements in social innovation may appear as a tautology, in practice, as we will see in the fourth section of this chapter, this role can be quite complex or even contradictory.

The local level as the tangible level of alternative development

Claims for alternative development emerge more easily at the local level: it is the locus and the privileged level of community identity, perception, and mobilization about local issues, and of resistance against alienating 'development' processes. Community sovereignty, autonomy, and solidarity receive their full meaning here, whereas at the individual or at the macro-economic level, they could appear as fully utopian.

As we have argued in Chapter 2, alternative development starts from the observation that local authorities and communities can play a relatively autonomous role and have a rather large space to manœuvre, with regard to global determinations (Autès 1997; Cox 1995; Klein and Lévesque 1995; Preteceille 1997). Articulation between local communities and global dynamics activates a process based upon the acceptance and defence of territorial differentiation and the recognition of diversity among the needs of local communities. Within French regional analysis, the notion of 'pays' reflects the idea of a multidimensional development model. Jean-Marc Ohnet (1996) has studied the historical trajectory of this concept:

Well before Fernand Braudel, Jean-François Gravier in his book 'Mise en Valeur de la France' (1948), recalled that national space is historically built from a weft of small homogeneous territorial units: the 'pays'. . . . The word 'pays' comes, as we all know, from the Gallo-Roman *pagus*. In fact, Gaul counted three hundred *pagi*. Through invasions, feudal divisions, the extraordinary administrative confusion of the Ancient Regime, the tribulations of districts and *arrondissements*, one distinguishes a kind of indestructible weft, hardly denser today than twenty centuries ago. (quoted by Ohnet 1996: 254)

In France, in 1995, the 'pays' was recognized by the spatial planning and development law (Loi d'orientation pour l'aménagement et le développement du territoire). The 'pays' is not considered as a territorial unit for public administration, but as a

space of social cohesion expressing 'a community of economic and social interests' [which] manifests itself in the first place as a 'relevant territory' (a 'territoire pertinent') to federate and rationalize strategies of economic development; . . . (Ohnet 1996: 255)

Other authors have used the same notion of 'pays' to express relations between economic, cultural, and political dynamics at the local level.[2]

If the local seems the privileged level for mobilizing for alternative development, this does not exclude the importance and the necessity of co-operation with agents outside the locality. Not only with respect to local mobilization, but also as far as the content of actions is concerned, external support is a necessary condition for greater efficacy and innovation. This idea is explicitly present in the model of Integrated Area Development which served as the analytical framework for research into the role of local development in the struggle against social exclusion within the European Union (Moulaert *et al.* 1994*a*).

4.3. Integrated Area Development: social innovation as a conditio sine qua non

4.3.1. Integrated Area Development: a synthesis for alternative local development?

The importance of individual experiences, the strong presence of practising planners among authors of local development, the various disciplinary orientations of researchers, the recent history of the study of local development: all

---

[2] For further discussion see Fathi 1996.

these factors explain the quite empirical and dispersed nature of the literature on local development (Moulaert and Demazière 1996*a*, 1996*b*). However, in this very socio-political domain, learning takes place through the comparative analysis of experiences in different countries, regions, communities, and through a variety of cultural, social, and political traditions (Moulaert *et al.* 1994*a*; Wilson, Moulaert, and Demazière 1997). To compare experiences of alternative development, there is need for a common reference framework. Recently, a number of efforts were made to elaborate a common 'reading guide' for local development (Wilson, Moulaert, and Demazière 1997). The study of the development of localities using the notion of 'local governance' and—although this is a more limited concept—'urban regime' has opened opportunities for a more coherent analysis of the relationships between politics, the economy, and society within urban and rural localities. Unfortunately, these contributions show only a theoretical interest in social inequality and exclusion within local societies. There is therefore a pressing need for research integrating urban governance into the dynamics of social integration and exclusion (Moulaert, Farcy, and Delvainquière 1996; Le Galès 1998). This integration would require a revisiting of the role of local and direct democracy, of socio-cultural associations and social movements, as well as *ad hoc* coalitions of local political, economic, and socio-cultural interests in governance (see the model of Integrated Area Development presented in Fig. 4.1).

The Integrated Area Development (IAD) approach is based on the idea that the development to be pursued in a locality should take into account its historical trajectory. From this perspective, history is reconstructed using a common regulationist categorical framework—see Chapter 3—for the analysis of the nature and causes of socio-economic disintegration and the potential for recovery. The fate of certain groups or the entire population is linked to the process of integration or disintegration of the locality (again see Chapter 3).

A detailed reading of the forces of decline and resurrection in each locality following the regulationist lexicon permits the identification not only of the mechanisms of disintegration, but also of the specific assets of each locality that would enable it to redevelop. For these assets fully belong to the dynamics of suffering and struggle against submergence. The preservation of traditional culture, the revival of traditional activities, the valorization of skills and professional experiences, social-cultural life, informal relationships in all sectors of social life, etc., are the vectors of local renaissance. It is within this existential melting pot that the dialectics of Integrated Area Development come to life.

4.3.2. Local development and the need for an integrated approach

The literature cited in the previous sections and the research on the localities for the European Commission show a great variety of local development

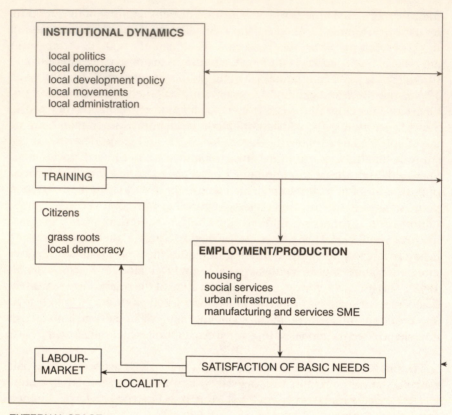

EXTERNAL SPACE

Fig. 4.1. Social integration and Integrated Area Development
Source: Moulaert, Delvainquière, and Delladetsima 1997.

practices (Moulaert *et al.* 1994*a*). At the level of analysis one manages easily to
distinguish alternative from orthodox models of development. But in practice
we find an impressive combination of orthodox principles (pure economic
growth, large-scale physical planning projects, deregulation of real estate and
labour-markets) and alternative principles (satisfaction of basic needs, direct
democracy for citizens and groups of excluded citizens, application of principles of self-management and self-production) as well as principles belonging
to different urban planning traditions (Master Plan, Strategic Plan, Integrated
Planning). From our research, we have observed both encouraging and discouraging elements for the future of alternative development strategies. A first
observation is that there exists a host of strategy domains and objectives.

Table 4.1 gives an overview of development planning domains and goals as
they were observed in the locality study for the European Commission. Five

domains were recognized: physical planning, cultural planning, economic development, labour-market, and social integration and protection. As can be observed from the figure, within each of these domains, several goals were identified. Such a myriad of strategy domains and objectives calls for the recognition of the specificity of each of the domains but at the same time there is a need to connect them to a general structuring principle to which we will return. A second observation is a dispersion of agency efforts. Table 4.2 ,which is even denser than Table 4.1, is an illustration of agencies involved in planning domains at the municipal or the city level only. This dispersal of competencies was quite discouraging from the point of view of an integrated approach to planning. On the basis of our sample, which contains only twenty-nine localities, we see that for the five planning domains almost forty different types of planning agencies are involved. This makes co-ordination and communication quite complex, of course.

Table 4.1. *Development planning domains and goals*

Physical planning	Cultural planning	Economic development	Labour-market	Social integration and protection
Land use Environmental upgrading Infrastructure (roads, communication) Housing	Cultural heritage protection Urban renovation Cultural programmes	Investment Diversification Restructuring of activities and firms Marketing	Education and training Insertion	Social services: health care, child care, assistance to the elderly, to the disabled

A third observation is that the budgetary philosophies for local development planning observed by localities are quite orthodox in nature, orthodoxy in this context meaning supporting, from an economic point of view, mainly high technology and professional services projects or, from the cultural and political point of view, supporting prestigious city-marketing investment, physical redevelopment, and revitalization programmes. We saw in Chapter 2 that these types of projects are not of much use to the segments of the population and to the deprived groups in which our approach is interested. A fourth general observation is that the relationship between social and economic policy is antagonistic. This is partly due to the predominance of economic targets in the local budget. If most of the money is drained away into prestigious economic and architectural programmes, then of course very little is left for social programmes to retrain the unskilled and for the housing of the homeless—or quasi-homeless—i.e. people with very poor quality housing. This antagonism—and we hope it is just a paradox—must be bridged if we want to come to an integrated approach to local development.

The fifth general observation is that the antagonistic relationship between social and economic policy weighs heavily on the relationship between the private and the public sector. The public sector, being up to now the main actor for social strategies and policies, sees itself more and more forced into a position where, in the name of the general interest, an increasing portion of public expenditure goes to the so-called economic restructuring and physical revitalization programmes (Moulaert, Swyngedouw, and Rodriguez (eds.) forthcoming). The sixth general observation concerns the relative powerlessness of the public sector. Competencies are dispersed, not only at the local level, but also between the local and other levels of the public sector. Moreover, and although this situation is improving rapidly, there is a lack of management and strategy skills and of financial resources to balance out the different domains of what is to become an integrated development action planning.

The last general observation about the development strategies in our sample localities is the denial of local potential. This may be the most 'disempowering' observation of what is going on in urban areas with severe disintegration problems. When mechanisms of socio-economic disintegration are at work, either collective pessimism and inertia prevail, or orthodox development models, which apparently lead to some positive results in other localities with less severe problems, are idealized and followed uncritically. Policy-makers and planners easily fall into the trap of 'imitating the impossible'. Localities with restructuring problems, which, according to NEP logic, are to become overnight a high level professional service centre, or to develop a CBD with a very strong export, financial exchange, and shipping infrastructure position, are the victims of unacceptable political and economic stress. It is as if their local possibilities are washed away by the severity of the crisis and the imposition of orthodox recipes based on high technology professionalism and large-scale physical reconstruction.

However, many so-called socio-economically disintegrated localities have strong local potential in terms of culture, the construction of social relations, tourism, and artisan activity. And even if activities in these fields are by themselves insufficient to solve severe unemployment problems, they should certainly be mobilized and included in an integrated area development approach. We know that the local potential should play a major role in this approach; and that the mobilization of local and 'extra' local resources supported by a community-rooted decision-making model, is a key factor of local development based on social innovation.

4.3.3. Integrated Area Development and social innovation

The main problem of disintegrated areas facing (re)development is disintegration and fragmentation among and within the various subsystems of the local society. In fact this fragmentation affects not only socio-economic activity, but also the living environment, civil society, and political life. Even if some problems of ineffective administration within the organization and the functioning of local public authorities are recognized as general, the atmosphere of decline seems to reinforce them. As we saw, specific problems for redevelopment strategies in disintegrated areas can be spelled out in terms of: a wide diversity of policy/action domains and objectives, the dispersion of agents and actions, contradictory strategic logic (and in the first place the contrast between economic and social, or socio-economic and ecological logic), the low weight given to the needs of the most deprived groups in urban society, and the underestimation of the (mobilizing) power of the 'local potential' (Moulaert, Delvainquière, and Delladetsima 1997).

The thesis which is defended here is that disintegrating forces and incoherence among strategy approaches should be overcome by putting the needs and the socio-political organization of deprived or excluded groups at the heart of local redevelopment strategies. The philosophy of the Integrated Area Development model is based on the satisfaction of basic needs. This satisfaction is achieved by the combination of several processes: the revealing of needs by grass-roots movements and through institutional dynamics, the integration of deprived groups into the labour-market and into local production systems (construction of housing, ecological production activities, urban infrastructure development, social services, SME for manufacturing and trade), and training permitting participation in the labour-market. Institutional dynamics play a predominant role in the process of empowerment that should lead to economic proactivity (Moulaert, Delvainquière, and Delladetsima 1997). Institutional dynamics nourish in a permanent way local democracy and relationships with local authorities and with other private and public partners situated outside the locality but participating in local development. The local community should take renewed possession of its own governance, thus putting its own movements central in the renaissance process (Martens 1996).

The thesis of Integrated Area Development is socially innovative in at least two senses. First, from a sociological point of view, it means innovation in the sense defined by Max Weber: innovation in the relations between individuals and between groups, and considered as different from technical innovation. Criticisms of 'innovation determined by technology' have been formulated by evolutionary economics (Dosi *et al.* 1988). But for the purpose of local development strategies, where innovation of social relations demands several actions, the view of innovation by these economists is not sufficiently social and organizational (Moulaert, Sekia, and Boyabé 1999). The organization of underprivileged groups, the establishment of communication channels between privileged and underprivileged citizens in urban society, and the creation of grass-roots democracy at the local level (neighbourhood, small communities, groups of homeless, long-term unemployed) play a key role in the innovation of social relations and are not analysed by evolutionary economics.

The second meaning of social innovation reinforces the first: it is the sense of social economy and also of social work. The challenge here is to satisfy the

Table 4.2. *Agencies involved in planning domains at the municipal (city) level*

Physical planning	Cultural preservation and progress	Economic development	Labour-market	Social integration and protection
Public	**Public**	**Public**	**Public**	**Public**
City physical planning department	City cultural department	City/regional economic development agencies	Employment agencies	Social service agencies (health centres, nurseries, . . .)
Environmental services	City urban renovation department	Chambers of commerce	Training and employment committees	Municipal welfare departments and agencies
City physical infrastructure department (roads, sewage system, . . .)	City technical departments	City/region commercial departments	Professional training centres	Homes and services for elderly, handicapped, . . .
Social housing providers	Cultural centres, museums, theatres		Labour law control administration	
			Schools and school boards	
Private	**Private**	**Private**	**Private**	**Private**
Land development corporations	Private cultural centres, museums, theatres	Private or privatised development companies	Most of the public institutions mentioned above have their private counterparts	Private service firms
Construction and real estate firms	Cultural foundations	Holdings, investment corporations		
		Grass-roots development associations		

basic needs of groups of citizens deprived of a minimum income, housing, access to quality education, and to the benefits of the information society.

The combination of both readings of social innovation stresses the importance of the creation of bottom-up structures for participation, decision-making, and production. The mobilization of political forces which will enable integrated development is based on the empowerment of citizens deprived of their most basic material, social, and political rights.

Examples of such alternative strategies were found in several localities in our study. A general overview of the most striking innovative actions is provided in Table 4.3. The examples given here illustrate several aspects of the double definition of social innovation. Vocational training is either meant to reintegrate the unemployed in the regular labour-market or in new production initiatives in the construction sector (several localities), consumer goods, and ecological activities (Hamburg). The satisfaction of basic needs is especially present in the mobilization of unemployed masons or other artisans in the construction of new housing or the upgrading of existing facilities. In many localities networking for production, training, and neighbourhood governance is explicitly present. In this way, several basic features of the Integrated Area Development model—see again Fig. 4.1—emerge in the case studies. We will deal with them in more detail in the case of Antwerp, Hamburg, Rostock, Girona, Charleroi, and Bilbao in Chapter 5.

In the next section we focus on the role of social movements in social innovation. Social movements are social change agents, because their emergence usually means a change in the social relations of development, but also because they are catalysts in the definition of basic needs and the modes in which they can be satisfied.

4.4. The specific role of social movements

For our purposes, it is essential to identify the processes that determine the origin, the life history, and the role of social movements in local development strategy.

Firstly, a historical approach is required. It is, for example, necessary to point out the transition of left-wing macro-movements on 'grand' themes such as civil rights in the USA (Fisher 1993) and social emancipation in Europe (Mayer 1995), towards more thematically focused movements such as neighbourhood committees or organizations that deal with education and social reintegration. It is also important to compare contemporary urban movements with those in the 1960s and 1970s, which often laid the foundations for today's co-operative initiatives (Topalov 1989; Castells 1975; Castells 1983; Vanden Eede and Martens 1994). The 'macro roots' of many among these micro-movements are historically clear, among them the neighbourhood committees in Antwerp that became inspired by the '1968 movement', and the

Table 4.3. *Illustrations of innovative initiatives in local development planning*

Retraining and integration into the labour-market (1)	New production initiatives (2)	Vocational training adapted to the needs and to the possibilities of the population (3)	Actions developing specific activities, answering to local needs, with potential new jobs for local people (4)	Strengthening of the local productive system (5)	Actions in favour of stronger links between economic strategies and social policies (6)	Improving housing and fighting poverty (7)	Agency networks for local economic development (8)	Development strategies—problematic implementation (9)
Hamburg job creation, training and education of jobless people for actual and future needs of the private economy	Rostock initiatives to support starters to go from protected employment to market participation	Valenciennes specialized professional training centres with the co-operation of a big firm located in the area		Roanne promotion of the local economy, amelioration of the educational and professional system	Barakaldo general conscience of the need for an integral intervention. Strong focus on social policy	Hamburg urban redevelopment strategies in the most deprived areas	Valenciennes local task force. Numerous and ambitious programmes	Rothopos no development strategies. Usually externally induced interventions with a destructive character
Dortmund retraining schemes especially for those employed in SMEs and technology	Hamburg initiatives to support starters	Comara Montes de Oca development of a stable training infra-structure	Hamburg job creation, training and education of jobless people for actual and future needs of the private economy	Ostiglia initiatives for comparative analysis, networking with other business services centres and localities involved in similar problems	NE Antwerp there is a framework of a global strategy to develop	Bremen job creation in urban areas which suffer big social problems (Quartiers en crises)	Barakaldo local task force. Many proposals	Agueda design of a development policy which reflects very limited skills. Problematic implementation

NE Antwerp training centre to new technologies

Bremen initiatives aiming at the incubation of new firms

Elgoibar training courses with a sectorial and experimental character

Dortmund specific activities aimed at a combination of environmentally and socially useful employment creation

Vigevano/Lomellina support of SMEs, business culture training, professional training

NE Antwerp advice on housing conversion or renovation

Lavrion local task force. Strong unionism

Sykies some kind of interventions only in urban planning

Charleroi remotivation and on-the-job training; support access to qualified jobs

Arganil initiatives for the creation of a vocational school oriented to the agro-forestry sector

Bremen job creation schemes: active labour-market policy

Urbania creation of a solidarity behaviour, promotion of the autonomy of local firms in the market

Gerona urban regeneration and housing strategies

Beira-Mar local task force. Not sufficient social sensitivity

Castres-Mazamet till 1991 no strategies for a new local development. Initiatives only for the amelioration of the education system

Fishguard vocational training for the local community

NE Antwerp setting-up of a firm which would provide specific services to big firms while hiring unqualified people

Charleroi foundation of a social housing society to intervene in social housing problems experienced by tenants

NE Antwerp innovation in partnership

Table 4.3. *cont.*

Retraining and integration into the labour-market (1)	New production initiatives (2)	Vocational training adapted to the needs and to the possibilities of the population (3)	Actions developing specific activities, answering to local needs, with potential new jobs for local people (4)	Strengthening of the local productive system (5)	Actions in favour of stronger links between economic strategies and social policies (6)	Improving housing and fighting poverty (7)	Agency networks for local economic development (8)	Development strategies—problematic implementation (9)
			Comarca Montes de Oca specific courses for the provision of social services in the locality				Rhondda innovation in partnership (Welsh Development Agency)	
							S. Cardiff innovation in partnership	

German cities where neighbourhood movements share common ecological principles with the ecologist or co-operative tradition.

Secondly, the historic reconstruction of social movements involved in contemporary socio-economic local development requires an ideological openness towards movements and large organizations honouring solidarity principles. Observation of the situation *sur le terrain* often shows the action of churches and of socio-cultural groups attached to, or operating in the margin of, political movements with a progressive, centrist, or conservative flavour. But it also shows protest movements animated by agents whose basic needs satisfaction is threatened or abolished. If the latter style is most in accordance with the logic of Integrated Area Development, in reality one observes that the social movements that are today most active in concrete development strategies are often not very clear on their ideological content. Many combine direct action-orientated logic with the style of reformist movements seeking to collaborate in an efficient way with local authorities.

One should object to a too simple analysis, one in the style of the 'life cycle of social movements' which can be characterized as 'in origin radical struggle—then a programme of political demands—next collaboration with local authorities—to finish with integration into social services or development agencies resulting from the collaboration with the local governance system'. This interpretation of the history of social movements absorbed in urban redevelopment is too mechanical and does not correspond to our findings. Their roles as critical observers and initiators of new policies do not preclude their close collaboration with local authorities. Real-life action models depend on the tradition of local governance (e.g. labour municipalities with a long tradition of collaboration with various social movements), the modes of integration of social innovators in local administration, the diversity of the action points, the diversification of collaborations, and the financial sources of movements. Even when long-time social movements transform themselves into 'Neighbourhood Development Corporations' or 'Integration Foundations', this does not mean that their role as radical social innovators disappears. It may even be the case that the opposite occurs: in a certain number of cases, through institutionalization, movements have managed to reduce their dependence upon the political organisms of local public administration or of funding agencies exerting too large an influence on the movements' programmes.

In general, despite radically different origins, basic needs satisfaction is essential for all social movements. A number of common features among the movements involved in local development have appeared in our research:

• institutional collaboration with public, semi-public, or private institutions (local, regional, national, European, etc.). This type of collaboration often results in partnerships established with associations, services, organizations responsible for social animation, and training and social economy production at the level of urban districts or neighbourhoods;

- professional co-operation with technicians, high level specialists, and engineers in various disciplines (architecture and construction, technology and organization consulting, human resources management, sociology and psychology, economics, administration and management);
- the adoption of models of efficient organization, management and production is another aspect of the new professional style of movements;
- 'reformism': certain originally more radical objectives of social movements have been altered as a result of specific political approaches or actions. Therefore, there is no obvious correlation between professionalization and radical reform strategies among social movements;
- protest against the alienation of initial objectives by the actual political practice involved. The 'life cycle' theory can help to illuminate this phenomenon. New social movements (criticizing reforms?) react against associations that seem to have 'lost their bearings'. In the case of grass-roots movements, reacting in the first instance to observed alienation, the seeds of the protest lie always with the neglect of basic needs (economic, social, and political);
- a representative function which is assured by radical movements or by institutionalized movements, which believe that their action model can be replicated in other local communities with similar problematic conditions;
- consultancy services which are available for marginal groups or active agents in order to support them in establishing their own initiatives;
- as a consequence of partnerships, local authorities often integrate agendas of social movements. Part of the 'personnel' of social movements becomes involved with development organizations created by the partnerships between movements and authorities. Local authorities often act as managers of these organizations, and also as their co-founder or 'external' controller—in the name of local democracy. This 'incorporation' of movement agendas often results in a twofold dynamics: consolidation of local development dynamics and a return to the grass-roots origin of many social movements. In fact, the latter gather themselves in a position of direct confrontation with the concerned population, which may provoke a political radicalization.

But the grass-roots content varies strongly among movements. The degree of involvement of the excluded citizens in social movements and local development associations varies significantly. The 'doing for' the excluded that is undertaken by the associations may signify a reproduction of paternalism, an abandoning of basic needs and the mechanisms of democratic decision-making and management.

4.5. Conclusion

There have been major deficiencies in the analysis and strategies of redevelopment of urban areas in decline. Analysis put too much stress on economic mechanisms. And when social, political, cultural, and ecological issues were involved, they were linked and subsumed under economic reasoning which therefore failed to grasp the importance of social dynamics in redevelopment strategies. As a consequence, the latter were formulated and implemented in an instrumentalist way, setting growth and investment objectives as a function of traditional policy instruments. Institutional dynamics were supposed to follow the political economic logic of urbanist regeneration, high technology production, business services, and the professional reskilling of the labour force.

The failure of many redevelopment strategies lies in this exogenous role reserved for social dynamics. As argued in this chapter, social dynamics are at the heart of 'community relevant' development strategies and social innovation is the engine that is required to make sputtering localities move along the lines of an Integrated Area Development project.

The Integrated Area Development model is integrated in several ways: it combines various development rationales, and integrates subsystems and spatial levels of development. It manages to direct the complexity of a project by structuring it around the principle of social innovation, which is not only defined in terms of the basic material needs of the concerned communities, but also by new modes of social organization by the grass-roots movements.

The model of Integrated Area Development—or comparable models—needs further examination and implementation. More evidence is needed from its implementation practice. And better links with socio-political action must be established. The latter can be done through communication and experience sharing between local authorities, development agents, and scientists working in this field of research. The following chapters contribute to these endeavours.

5

Experiences in Integrated
Area Development

This chapter examines first the mechanisms of social exclusion and socio-economic disintegration in six specific cities (Antwerp, Hamburg, Rostock, Charleroi, Bilbao, and Girona) and their selected neighbourhoods. Second, the strategies in these cities for local redevelopment and social reintegration, from the perspective of the Integrated Area Development model, are scrutinized. Third, the chapter offers a brief evaluation of the governance dynamics in each of these localities, especially with respect to their relationship to alternative development strategies.

With the exception of Girona, which has a more hybrid economic basis, these cities were selected from a list of cities whose socio-economic fate and future have for several centuries been significantly determined by the predominance of one group of economic activities (port activities, steel and metal industry, coal mining), and that have shown courageous and creative experiences with supplementary or alternative redevelopment strategies, at least in certain neighbourhoods.

Table 5.1 summarizes the types of dominant economic sectors present in each city. It also mentions the specific neighbourhoods that were studied and the fundamental problems reflecting the alienation of basic needs.

The first section in this chapter summarizes the debate on the New Economic Policy (NEP) at the urban level (cf. Chapter 1), the process of socio-economic disintegration in the selected neighbourhoods, and the need to anticipate specific development strategies as an appropriate mix of general and specific development perspectives (Chapters 3 and 4). In the second section, the basic needs alienated by economic decline and the restructuring process in each locality, as well as the creative mechanisms that will eventually allow redevelopment strategies, are examined.

The third section of the chapter provides more detail on 'new' socio-economic initiatives and how they are used to counter urban social and economic decline. We verify the validity of the Integrated Area Development approach by means of examples of multidimensional actions in each of the six cities. In the fourth section, governance dynamics are evaluated as to their social innovation content. Questions such as 'Are the urban and neigh-bourhood institutional dynamics supportive or integrated into the local

Table 5.1. *The case-study cities: their socio-economic structure and neighbourhood problems*

City population	Neighbourhood population	Socio-economic structure of the area/neighbourhood	Alienation of basic needs
Antwerp 1970: 550,146 1993: 462,336	Noord-Oost Antwerpen 1970: 43,661 1993: 33,466	Broken links with port activities Docking activity becomes increasingly labour saving while TNCs (chemical industry mainly) hire professionals outside the area Suburbanization of the well-off population; arrival or consolidation of 'victims' of economic restructuring	Housing quality—physical decay
Hamburg 1975: 1,700,000 1996: 1,700,000	Hamburg-Mitte	City centre has been expensively and sometimes lavishly renovated (service and housing functions) Low-income groups forced to remain or move to downgraded inner-city areas	Housing quality
Bilbao 1975: 911,143 1996: 887,977	Barakaldo 1975: 117,747 1996: 100,474	Decline of steel and related industry: loss of 75% of industrial and 56% of total employment in 1980s. Strong impact on income generation	Minimum income—social services—housing quality—environmental decay
Girona 1991: 68,556	Torre Gironella 1991: 997 Font de la Polvora: 2677 Vila-Roja: 1424 Barri Vell: 2859	Small manufacturing and service jobs	Limited social infra-structure, low pensions for elderly
Charleroi 1977: 227,000 1993: 206,000	All neighbourhoods are considered. The spatial structure of the conurbation is heterogeneous. Some former mining districts are spatially and socially isolated. There is also a concentration of socially excluded people in the 19th-century core	Endless deindustrialization and very slow tertiarization. 40,000 jobs lost in the 1970s and 25,000 in the 1980s	Housing quality Pollution problems Health problems High number of minimex receivers
Rostock 1970: 200,000 1998: 207,000	Kröperliner Tor Vorstadt 1998: 13,674	19th-century residential area, affected by industrialization (1930s, 1950s) and deindustrialization dynamics (as of reunification)	Urban decay Housing quality 20% unemployment (1996)

Source: Case studies, local statistical data.

development strategies, or should they rather be considered as obstacles to socially innovative development trajectories?' are treated in the final section of the chapter.

5.1. Local socio-economic exclusion and theoretical analysis: a brush-up from previous chapters

The cities/neighbourhoods in our study have gone through a series of processes of economic restructuring, rising unemployment, and increasing social exclusion. There has been an evolution from a strategy of preserving industrial activity in the 1970s and 1980s, to the development of new activities with high productivity and export capacity. New development strategies were articulated around services and activities that would matter in the future (electronics, telecommunications, advanced producer services). The 'new' general agenda of local development was then to achieve a modern, innovative, and dynamic local production system, including the most advanced producer services based on the adaptation of the local structure to the exigencies of the new phase of global economic growth. This agenda was meant to be applicable to all localities in need of restructuring.

Yet localities have encountered a number of obstacles to an effective transformation of their local productive system. In previous chapters, we underlined the risks entailed in restructuring localities when strictly 'orthodox' economic strategies of local development are applied. This has meant a technocratic approach to leadership and public sector involvement, and an artificially supported disequilibrium in political choices and public spending in favour of actions strictly oriented towards the market economy. It leads to prioritizing the use of public money in favour of capital intensive business activities and physical regeneration, feeding antagonisms between social and economic policies. The negative impact of such development strategies on disintegrated areas is visible in at least two ways. First, the lack of multidimensionality of the planning process leads to disregarding local basic needs, especially of certain groups or neighbourhoods; secondly, technocratic and professional myopia kills opportunities for renewed democracy in impoverished neighbourhoods by excluding large parts of the local population from the new economic growth.

A broad and coherent analytical perspective was designed to analyse the social, political, economic, and cultural structures of socio-economically disintegrated areas or localities (Chapter 3), and to identify local development strategies responding to their main socio-economic problems and with the potential to establish new solid developing strategies which can address the basic needs of these localities (Chapter 4). Thus we conclude that the way the productive system is meeting local demand in terms of social integration in each locality questions the limits of the traditional strategies and the necessity to design new innovative policies, especially for disintegrated localities.

5.2. Local crisis formation and its repercussions

The theoretical analysis in Chapter 3 suggests the need for detailed empirical research of each locality according to a general logic designed to allow for comparison and to enable conclusions with respect to development perspectives. Such an approach highlights the main mechanisms that are responsible for socio-economic disintegration and points to the domains where proactive strategies to counter the disintegration process must be designed. Of course, economic disintegration plays a major role in the explanation of the socio-economic problems of each locality. But the strategic response of the local communities to their problems is, among other things, dependent on the social cohesiveness of local production systems, their embeddedness in the regional and national societies, and the quality of their institutional system (Moulaert, Leontidou *et al.* 1994*a*). Differences in the intensity of the restructuring crises in these localities can be classified using four variables already explained and illustrated in Chapter 3 for the larger group of localities. The first two are the degree of diversification in the sectoral structure and the urban versus rural character of the locality that characterize economic development. The last two, i.e. the cohesion of the local production system and the level of responsiveness of the planning agents and the local institutions to the restructuring problems, require a sociological and political reading of local dynamics. In this chapter, we concentrate on the first, third, and fourth variables.

5.2.1. The degree of diversification of the sectoral structure

Manufacturing industry in all these localities has undergone important changes in its production structure and labour relationships. Localities with a predominance of steel and coal industries and a strong tradition of specialized and unionized labour, such as Charleroi and Bilbao, have suffered tremendous job losses. Laid-off workers from these industries are rarely incorporated into new economic activities and, in fact, have a higher probability of remaining in long-term unemployment than either skilled redundant workers from Fordist industries (e.g. automobile) or green-field labour. Modes of organization used in the traditional industries of these localities can only partly be reapplied in new service or manufacturing activities with a flexible production system based on polyvalent labour skills.

Table 5.2 provides key statistics on the shifts in sectoral structure over the period 1970–95. At this decentralized spatial scale, statistics are hardly comparable in time and definition but, none the less, they provide an indication of how severe restructuring problems are.

Table 5.2. *The case-study cities: employment per sector and unemployment 1970s–1990s*

City	Sectoral structure of total employment 1970	Sectoral structure total employment 1995	Shifts in socio-economic structure of district: main indications (1970–95)	Unemployment
Antwerp (urban region)	Secondary: 153,000 (45.8%) Services: 180,000 (53.9%) Total: 334,000 (100%)	Secondary: 108,000 (30.6%) Services: 244,000 (69.1%) Total: 353,000 (100.0%)	**District: North-east Antwerp** Drop in active population 40%, stronger than the loss of population in the district (−22%) Decline of the main activity, i.e. retail trade; increase in unemployment Sharp increase in the proportion of foreign population (5.3% in 1970; 28% in 1993)	City 　1970: 1.9% 　1995: 11.1% District 　1970: 2.5% 　1995: 18.4%
Hamburg	Secondary: 348,100 (1.1%) Services: 607,300 (62.8%) Total: 966,300 (100%)	Secondary: 196,800 (21.6%) Services: 715,900 (77.8%) Total: 919,600 (100%)	**District: Hamburg-Mitte** Over the last 15 years, service employment increased by 40%; employment dropped by 12% in trade and transport and 23% in manufacturing	City 　1970 = 0.4% 　1995 = 10.7% Districts in 1995: varies between under 4% and over 8.5%
Metropolitan Bilbao	Secondary: 169,128 (57%) Services: 124,943 (42.1%) Total: 296,480 (100%)	Secondary[a]: 92,177 (41.1%) Services: 176,025 (65.3%) Total: 269,528 (100%)	**Barakaldo** During the 1980s, this locality lost 75% of its manufacturing employment; more than half of this loss occurred between 1985 and 1993. Moreover, in contrast with the aggregate performance for the metropolitan area, service employment fell by 12%. As a result, between 1981 and 1993, Barakaldo lost 56% of its total employment	*Metropolitan Bilbao* 　1975: 2.3% 　1995: 23.4% *Barakaldo* 　1970: 2.9% 　1995: 30.1%

Girona	(1990) Secondary: 20.7% Services: 78.7%	**Vila-Roja and Font de la Plovora** Areas with a fragile economic basis. A combination of various exclusion factors: illiteracy, poor quality public housing. In Font de la Polvora, 70% of population are gipsies	City 8.63% (1991)
Rostock	Hansestadt Rostock 1996 Secondary sector: 23.64% Services: 74.76% Total: 94,879	Estimates for the District (Bezirk) in 1969 Primary: 18.0% Secondary: 35.1% Services: 46.9% Total: 123,833	**Kröperliner Tor Vorstadt** Decline of traditional trade and artisan activities. Rupture of links with harbour complex	City 1970: 0% 1998: 21% District 1998: 20%
Charleroi	(1990) Secondary: 41,300 (36.7%) Services: 70,400 (62.5%) Total: 112,600 (100%)	(1974) Secondary: 96,900 (59.4%) Services: 65,000 (39.9%) Total: 163,000 (100%)	**City** Crisis and restructuring of heavy industry More modern industries like electronics and aeronautics have also reduced their number of employees	City 1974: 4.4% 1995: 24.1%

Notes:
[a] Data for 1996.
The secondary sector includes manufacturing plus construction.
Data for the primary sector can be obtained by deduction.

In Charleroi, processes of industrial restructuring during the second half of the 1970s led to plant closures (in the iron and steel industry, machine manufacturing, etc.), a strong and steady decrease of industrial employment, and almost purely defensive strategies on the part of surviving firms (Demazière 1997). However, the sector base of the local economy has registered very little change: today the steel industry is still the biggest local employer and the city has the weakest service economy in urban Belgium. Derelict industrial sites and deprived districts, with serious problems for their population, are major features of Charleroi's urban condition and image (the 'black land').

Employment destruction in manufacturing is one of the more visible results of economic crisis in Charleroi. Since 1974, the city has lost more than 40,000 jobs, pushing its unemployment rate from 4.4 per cent in that year to around 25 per cent in the mid-1990s, the second highest in Belgium (Demazière 1997). Furthermore, a large portion of the unemployed population in Charleroi is struck by extreme poverty (12 per cent). In the early 1990s, the number of minimum income receivers among the local population rose from 900 in 1976 to 1,600 in 1981 and to 4,200 in 1993. Besides, average income per capita is much lower in Charleroi than in any of the other large cities in the country: it amounts to 6,380 ECU versus 6,710 in Brussels, 6,970 in Liège, 7,160 in Ghent, and 7,540 in Antwerp (for the 1992 fiscal year).

In Bilbao, one of the main urban industrial centres and the most important cargo harbour within Spain, two decades of severe manufacturing decline, plant closures, demographic stagnation, and loss of centrality functions have transformed it into an archetype of a declining industrial area. Between 1975 and 1996, metropolitan Bilbao lost almost half (47 per cent) of its manufacturing employment, mainly in traditional industries such as shipbuilding, steel manufacturing, metal products, basic chemicals, and electric equipment. During the same period, the growth of the service sector (+ 50,000 jobs) only partially offset job losses in manufacturing, but it raised its share of total employment from 42.1 per cent to 65.3 per cent while the share of industrial employment dropped from 45.5 per cent to 26.9 per cent. However, total employment in 1996 still remained below 1975 levels and unemployment rates were as high as ever, close to 30 per cent for the metropolitan area as a whole.

Changes in total and sector employment have not taken place in a homogeneous manner within metropolitan Bilbao. Economic restructuring has affected different localities of the urban region in diverse ways and levels of intensity. Municipalities on the left bank of the river, an enclave of large heavy manufacturing firms and working-class neighbourhoods, have suffered the brunt of manufacturing decline. As a result, they not only have the highest levels of unemployment, poverty, and marginalization but also of physical decay, environmental degradation, and housing problems. In 1986, 82 per cent of jobs in the iron and steel, metal transformation, precision mechanics, and the chemical industry were located in this area. Today, large firms still account for over 70 per cent of total industrial employment. Barakaldo, the second largest municipality on the left bank, is one of the worst hit by industrial plant closures and job loss and, consequently, by social exclusion. During the 1980s, this locality not only lost 75 per cent of its industrial employment but, in contrast to aggregate performance for the metropolitan area, service employment also fell by 12 per cent. As a result, between 1981 and 1993, Barakaldo lost 56 per cent of its total employment[1] (see Rodríguez *et al.* 1994).

Patterns of social and territorial polarization and exclusion are also evidenced by intra-metropolitan population dynamics. Since 1981, the metropolitan population has steadily declined, losing, between 1981 and 1991, close to 30,000 people, i.e. 3.1 per cent of total population. But while left bank municipalities suffered a steady diminution of population during this decade, the right bank areas registered a significant increase both in absolute and relative terms, benefiting from intra-metropolitan population flows from the left to the right bank areas, which are much better off (Martínez and Vicario 1997). Finally, increasing income inequality has been an integral part of deindustrialization dynamics but with very differentiated impacts within the urban region. For example, between 1982 and 1992, the average income of Barakaldo *vis-à-vis* the metropolitan area fell from 88 per cent to 80 per cent; in the meantime, the average income of the wealthier localities in the right bank jumped from 128 per cent to 141 per cent of the average index.

In the case of Hamburg, the biggest harbour and the second largest city in Germany (1.7 million inhabitants), de-industrialization affected particularly the port economy, which dragged down other activities in the city and the surrounding areas. Following the peak of its economic development in the 1960s, the agglomeration experienced an acute crisis in the 1970s, with shipyard closures, decline in shipping and trading activities, and out-migration of local harbour firms. In 1987 unemployment reached 13.7 per cent and despite a temporary downswing at the turn of the decade has remained since then a structural problem.

As a first reaction to the crisis, the Federal Government urged the *Land* government towards a more conventional strategy focusing on the regeneration of the traditional economic structure. This meant basically an attempt to modernize the port activities (through investment in container terminals and related infrastructure) and to attract new shipping industries and services. This strategy, however, did not produce the expected results and did not tackle the acute unemployment problem; moreover, it led to an escalating growth in public debt (in 1983 it amounted to 20 per cent of public income).

The early 1980s, with the coming into power of the new municipal administration, marked a shift in the overall economic strategy for the agglomeration.

---

[1] None the less, the shift away from manufacturing activities is quite intense. While in 1986 the industrial sector employed 52.7% of total employment in Barakaldo and the service sector 47%, in 1991 the weight of services increased to 53.7% while the share of industry fell to 45.9%. Also, in 1992, out of 141 licences issued by the municipality for new economic activities, only 4 of them were for industrial establishments.

The new strategy focused on the development of tourism, high technology industries, and producer services. This change should be considered as the outcome of the failure of the previous policy and the political line of the new administration, combined with the transformations in Eastern Europe (and especially the then DDR) that have influenced the economy of Hamburg due (among other factors) to its strategic geographic position. The positive effects of the new strategy began to be felt by the late 1980s with increases in the gross net product (5.45 per cent) and in service sector employment.

Hamburg came relatively unscathed through the recession period of the early 1990s, since it benefited from the unification process, assuming the role of a major supplier of goods and services to the new German states. Hamburg's transactions with the new states increased by 76 per cent against an average of 45 per cent for the western states (Häussermann *et al.* 1993*a*). However, the effects of the crisis have been felt later on, bringing to the surface the issues of unemployment, social polarization, and deprivation.

The emphasis placed on service sector development and new manufacturing activities did not exert any significant influence on the unemployment problem. Unemployment reached its peak in 1987 (13.9 per cent). By 1991, although significantly reduced, the unemployment rate in Hamburg (8.6 per cent) was still far above the national average (6.0 per cent). In 1996 it again reached 11.4 per cent. Hamburg could be considered as a typical case of a growth economy without employment creation ('jobless growth'). In 1996 the Lawaetz-Stiftung pointed out that 'the gross domestic product in Hamburg has risen by about 30% over the last 15 years, while the number of people employed—with some slight intermediate fluctuations—is found equal to that of 1980' (Häntsch and Schmalriede 1996).

The increase of GDP per capita could easily allow for redistribution of income. But the 'global' inclination towards no redistribution (see Chapters 2 and 6) seems to be very true in Hamburg. In this way also, the benefits of the economic strategy did not 'trickle down' to the weaker and deprived population strata such as the young, the elderly, women, and migrant populations (Turks, Poles, migrants from former Yugoslavia, Iranians, and, later on, migrants from the new German states). The adverse effects (unemployment, reduced incomes, and poverty) were particularly reflected in escalating homelessness, and the failure of the low-cost housing sector.

The effects of the economic development left a specific geographical imprint. This involved increasing population mobility problems and polarization among urban districts and neighbourhoods. The latter is reflected in the significantly lower income growth rate in the inner districts of Hamburg (Hamburg and Hamburg-Mitte and especially St Pauli) than in the northern part (Eimsbüttel) or the East Bergedorf to the south. The same applies when indicators reflecting social deprivation (earnings related benefits, unemployment benefits, and social welfare benefits) are taken into consideration. Again the most deprived district of the conurbation proves to be Hamburg-Mitte while the most prosperous one is Bergedorf. Finally a gentrification process seems to concentrate in areas such as Rotherbaum, Eimsbüttel, Eppendorf, and Winterhude. The area which faces acute downgrading problems is Wilhemsburg (Häussermann *et al.* 1993*a*).

Before reunification Rostock's role as a maritime centre for the former DDR was similar to Hamburg's in West Germany. As a leading *Hansestadt*—Member of the Hanseatic League—Rostock had played a significant economic role in medieval Europe. With the decline of the sailing ship trade, Rostock lost its leading role in Germany, and only returned to economic glory in the 1930s, in part because of its role in aircraft production. This industry was destroyed after the war. But, under the socialist regime, shipbuilding, engineering, and manufacturing continued to play a significant role. The maritime sector with related services was reinforced, and a fishing fleet was also maintained. With the unification process the strategic harbour and trade functions were lost. Today the conditions which sustained the growth and development of the conventional economic sectors have collapsed. The free market economy, selling off or closing down a large number of plants with high quality engineering experience, created high level unemployment. The confrontation with the 'open market' also revealed such issues as over-aged capital stock, labour training and retraining needs, the urge towards (new) management practices, etc.

In 1989 transportation and communication constituted 13.6 per cent of total employment for the region as a whole and 21 per cent in the city (in 1996 the figure for the city was 23.5 per cent). Other activities complementary to the maritime sector such as machine and vehicle construction represented 10 per cent of the regional and 13 per cent of the urban employment structure. As a result of the crisis, employment dropped between 1990 and 1993 by about 35 per cent. This particularly affected the large industrial complexes, while the SMEs that were established later could only partly absorb redundant labour. Under the circumstances unemployment escalated and by 1990 reached 17.6 per cent particularly affecting the weaker strata of the population such as women and young people (Schubert 1995).

However, by the end of 1992 the Rostock agglomeration began to exhibit signs of a relative recovery. This was due to the 'positive effect' of strong labour out-migration flows (migration towards western labour-markets amounted to 16,700 people, most of them young), the implementation of various vocational programmes and retraining schemes, and the expansion in job creation activities in the primary and secondary labour-markets. Thus by 1992 unemployment had dropped to 14 per cent (13 per cent in 1995) which was considerably below the average for the *Länder* (15.5 per cent). Thereafter Rostock followed the general employment crisis in Germany and by 1998 the unemployment rate was up to 20 per cent. In spite of the economic transformations, the maritime complex of the agglomeration, including shipbuilding, maritime trade, shipping transport, and fisheries, remained the stronghold of the local economy, although its share was considerably reduced (Schubert 1995, 1998). This also explains why the economic structure of the city remains extremely sensitive to boom-and-bust cycles.

Rostock's geography reflects a sharp unevenness in urban social development. The residential areas built prior to the First World War suffered from rapid industrialization, while the 'structural breakdown' after reunification has hampered the renewal of housing stock and the creation of local firms. The case-study area, Kröperliner Tor Vorstadt, located west of the historical centre, suffers from the moving-out of better-off families. Unemployment in this area corresponds to the city average (20 per cent), but physical infrastructure problems are particularly bad.

As the second city of Belgium (500,000 inhabitants) and the second port of Western Europe, Antwerp is a very significant economic pole. The ensemble of activities located on the port's territory (distribution and stocking, manufacturing production, private services, public sector) represent 3.5 per cent of the GNP of Belgium, more than either the contribution of domestic agriculture or the textile industry to the GNP. Manufacturing rests on the huge plants owned by General Motors, Ford, BASF, Bayer, and Exxon. In the Antwerp urban region, employment progressed by 5.7 per cent between 1972 and 1992 (from 334,000 to 353,000), against a decline of total employment in Belgium of 7 per cent. But the contribution of manufacturing industry to the Antwerp economy dropped considerably. In 1972 there were 153,000 manufacturing jobs; twenty years later this was down to 108,000, a decline of 29.4 per cent. The only exception is the chemical industry, which has virtually maintained its level of employment (about 23,000 jobs), and has kept Antwerp in position as the second chemical industry city in the world (after Houston). Metal industry employment went down from 53,000 to 34,000 (−35.8 per cent). The building industry, which witnessed a spectacular expansion in the 1960s, lost 5,000 jobs (from 24,000 to 19,000). In the same period salaried employment in services grew from 180,000 to 244,000.

Therefore, despite the economic crisis in many Western countries, the Antwerp economy has continued to grow. But this growth process has been accompanied by a social and spatial polarization of the urban region, such as in north-east Antwerp (36,000 inhabitants), a neighbourhood bordering the old historical centre. Built in the second half of the nineteenth century, this working-class and retail trade neighbourhood has suffered economic, social, and physical decline for many decades. The area now counts among its inhabitants, relatively speaking, many more unemployed and many less graduates than the rest of the city or the urban region. The housing stock, mainly private, is old, lacks comfort, and needs renovation. A significant part of the population, often of foreign origin, suffers from deprivation. Because of limited income growth, the local supply of consumer services has decreased over the last fifteen years.

The expansion of the service industry and the small weight of industry in the economy of Girona (12 per cent of total employment) has meant that the eminently industrial character of the economic crisis has, on the whole, hardly affected this area. Its unemployment rate in 1991 (8.63 per cent) was lower than in the region of Catalonia (11 per cent) and in Spain (15.60 per cent). However, the impact of the crisis on the industry in Girona has been important due to such factors as insufficient specialization, low levels of technological innovation, a down-scaling of firms, and the concentration of those production activities which exhibit a weak demand and labour-intensive processes (mechanical industries, meat industries, paper manufacturers, and specialized chemical industries). Thus, despite the fact that the largest part of the unemployed lost jobs in the service sector, the rate of unemployment in manufacturing is higher than that in services. For example, in 1990, 95 per cent of the manufacturing workers were affected by 'expedientes de regulacion', an administrative procedure used by the firms in periods of insolvency or crisis. The impact has been particularly severe in some of the more deprived neighbourhoods in the city: Torre Gironella, Font de la Polvora, Vila-Roja, and Barri Vell. Unemployment now adds to other social problems among the poor population of Villa-Roja and Font de la Polvora, including high illiteracy rates, low skill levels, citizen insecurity, and urban decay. The nature of the dominant sectors and the degree of diversification have obviously had an impact on the severity of the crisis. Besides, the significant proportion of precarious jobs, especially among women and seasonal workers, undermines the potential benefits of a high share of service sector activity.

5.2.2. Cohesiveness of the local production system

The cohesiveness of the local production system determines, to a large extent, the degree of integration or disintegration of urban society and its communities. This cohesion depends on several factors: the endogenous calibre of production factors and forces, the modes of organization of local production, the business culture, the links with the 'outside world' (trade, inward and outward investment, migration and commuting, inter-place networking). Of course, the cohesiveness of the local production system also depends strongly on the quality of the local institutions and the relations between them, as shown in section 5.2.3.

The cohesiveness of the local economy is strongly dependent on the history of its sectoral structure. Our six case-study areas are considered as of average 'cohesiveness'. But cohesiveness has a double face. It can foster change dynamics, but also block new initiatives. For example, the weight of long-standing industrial traditions in a mono-production system can paralyse the possibilities to organize new activities. And this may be the case in localities (e.g. Charleroi and Barakaldo) dominated for over a century by heavy industry, or localities built on a (significantly endogenous?) flexible industrial district pattern (see Amin and Robbins 1992).

The production system in Girona is mainly endogenous. The concentration of local small and medium-sized firms in the area plays a leading role in the devel-

Table 5.3. *Cohesiveness of local production systems*

City	Production system	Disintegrating forces	Factors of (renewed) cohesion
NE Antwerp	Part of the larger Antwerp economy, with small consumer-oriented business Strong interaction between endogenous development potential and inward investment by TNCs	Negative impact of global competition on job creation	One of the strongest local economic systems of Belgium Proactive and co-operative institutions
Hamburg	Externally induced growth model (trade, investment, . . .)	Strong stress on traditional paths of production and trade Public budget cuts	Strong growing economy with increasing disparities Jobless growth
Bilbao (Barakaldo)	Part of broader production system, few large firms with network of subcontractors	'Mono' industrial structure Absence of relation-ships between SME Heavy industry business culture	Growing involvement by local, regional, and central authorities in socio-economic support for the area
Girona	SME economy with endogenous character, today predominantly in services	Traditional industrial activities with skills and modernization problems	Dynamic local institutional system responsible for growing interaction between firms
Rostock	Traditional 'old' local production system (shipyard, port-related activities)	Poorly developed R. & D. potential Bypassed educational system	Public/private networks to cope with unemployment, training, investment, . . .
Charleroi	Disintegrated steel and metal manufacturing system	Complete loss of industrial dynamism Heavy industry business culture	Large-scale mobilization of local actors/ institutions for reconversion of the area

Source: Moulaert, Leontidou and Delladetsima eds. 1994.

opment of the service industry and allows them to establish local links within the urban market, which protect against volatile economic cycles. However, the sheltered character of the Girona economy seems to be threatened from within: (i) a labour-intensive economy, specializing in sectors with a weak demand, could lead to a loss of competitiveness with the outside world; (ii) low skilled human resources could hamper the modernization of these firms; (iii) the high salary of qualified workers may lead to cost inflation and affect the competitive position;

(iv) the nearly exclusive concentration of exporting activity with a small number of industrial multinational firms leads to a lack of opening to the outside market.

Most localities in our sample—with the exception of Girona—have been dominated by just a few heavy industries or clusters of activities. One of the most powerful experiences of a locality paralysed by its heavy industry history is that of Charleroi in Belgium, where the traditional industries have completely vanished and the active population is segmented in many different ways. In the case of Charleroi, there has never been a local entrepreneurial spirit. Only timid private efforts were made to diversify the local economy as the steel plants and coal-mines entered their fatal crisis. This crisis did not affect only blue-collar employment, since white-collar employment and self-employment also decreased in this locality throughout the 1980s and 1990s, whereas the latter remained stable or even increased in Wallonia (Belgium). Furthermore, the reduced skilled workforce and the low dynamism of the labour-market are two of Charleroi's main difficulties in the development of a coherent local socio-economic system. The city experiences difficulties in breaking through the monolithic business organization of its glorious past, and replacing it with SME networks.

Antwerp and Hamburg seem to suffer less from a lack of modernization in their economy, since their wider economic base offers stronger potential for diversity and the combination of various production systems provides a greater variety of modes of cohesiveness. The diversification of economic activity in general and of manufacturing industry in particular has produced uneven networks with specific professional and sectoral specialization, from which new initiatives, even in the alternative or 'socio-economy' sphere, can be developed. This may explain why these two urban economies managed to produce an organizational flexibility, whereas Bilbao failed to do so and sought for change through its traditional manufacturing and sectoral or professional networks. Despite the impossibility of studying the situation of Barakaldo as an isolated area because of the existence of strong economic links within the municipalities of the metropolitan area, there are some distinct quantitative and qualitative features that allow us to consider Barakaldo as a specific area in decline. Local production activities in Barakaldo are strongly dependent on a few conglomerates in the iron and steel industry, to which a large number of small and medium-sized firms are linked. The control of these conglomerates is mainly in the hands of the public sector or foreign investors. In contrast, SMEs are mostly locally owned and controlled. Industrial restructuring has affected these SMEs by forcing them, like the large corporations, to rationalize and reorganize or, at worst, to close down. The final result has been a reduction in the average size of firms within the area. At the same time, the low internationalization levels of Basque firms (in 1989, only 24.1 per cent of Basque firms registered some form of export activity but 68.9 per cent of small and medium-sized firms exported less than 20 per cent of their sales) tends to limit the creation of co-operative relations between firms. Yet, specific strategies based on inter-firm co-operation could allow firms to benefit from opportunities provided by European integration and the creation of a single unified market.

The shipbuilding sector, the port-related activities, and the fishing fleet, as already mentioned, have dominated Rostock's traditional local industry. Modern industrial branches, service sector development, R. & D. activities, let alone SMEs, did not form part of the economic development rationale of the socialist regime. Moreover, no middle class, which in most economies runs the artisan and trade sector, was developed. Thus the subsequent crisis situation has been conditioned by a characteristic of the former centrally planned economy: the compliance of the local economy and society to a single production system (big national shipping and industrial complexes).

As this system was forced into market capitalism, and lost its traditional markets, it not only dragged down the economy of the conurbation but also its entire institutional and social structure. Steeped in the tradition of central government administration, and lacking an entrepreneurial middle class, opportunities for recovery and development were initially not perceived as being a local matter. Rather, they were expected to come from outside Rostock, under the impetus of the 'new' state. But such expectations could hardly be met in an environment where state firms were compulsorily privatized, often by selling them to direct competitors.

The creation of an entrepreneurial milieu lies at the heart of Rostock's recovery and reconstruction. This involves long-term as well as short-term actions embracing public institutions, firms, and labour. Initiatives tackling unemployment and leading to the formation of self-sustained economic units in a new regional context receive a particular emphasis. In this respect also the former big corporations have a role to play by offering land, capital, and personnel. *Beschäftigungs und Qualifizierungsgesellschaften* (societies for employment and qualification) thus change from being fire-fighting institutions to becoming the promoters of regional economic development (Häussermann *et al.* 1993a, 1993b).

The possibility for renewed development in a locality depends strongly on the recovery or further enhancement of local cohesion. Among the fundamental principles feeding renewal feature professional synergies within and between economic activities, training and learning by exchange among firms, integration into broader spatial networks, and the rediscovery of local business traditions and culture. Localities whose economic development has rested on a monolithic economic structure (Charleroi, Bilbao-Barakaldo, Rostock) have problems fostering these new network dynamics. Cities like Antwerp and Hamburg with a wide variety of activity clusters, or Girona with a long-standing SME tradition, are maybe better placed to generate innovative organizational dynamics. However, the future of local development is also dependent on institutional dynamics.

5.2.3. Responsiveness of local agents and the institutional system

Localities with a disintegrated production system seem to have limited social and political mobilization power for the design and implementation of new local development strategies, which fall beyond the scope of existing industrial traditions. We saw in Chapter 3 that localities with comparable spatial and functional cohesiveness in their production system show different development capacities defined according to four variables: (i) the public institutional system; (ii) the quality of the local authorities; (iii) the collaboration between different public and private agents; and (iv) the involvement of the European Union.

Most of the six metropolitan areas in our study have well-established and skilful public authorities. However, these share the burdens of a complex administrative system, the 'urban fiscal crisis', and a lack of experience with decentralized production systems, social economy initiatives, and public–private partnerships. The latter often implies that the private sector frequently picks out the fruits from among the burdens carried by the public. Institutional proactivity of local authorities is mortgaged by an institutional and socio-economic past that cannot be easily figured away.

Within a larger political framework involving regional, national, and European partners, the municipal councils of certain localities play a small role in effective decision-making, as is the case of Charleroi. The setting up of alternative strategies undertaken by various local institutions has proved insufficient to resolve social and economic problems; training programmes provided by public training centres do not seem to help significantly to counteract the low dynamism of the labour-market (Van Doren 1996). In the case of Rostock's ex-socialist system, the entire institutional setting confined by the *Kombinate*, i.e. the education system, the health care system, and even housing provision, still proves to be inadequate.

But some of the case studies show a number of very interesting models of collaboration between different spatial levels in the political system. For example, Hamburg's local government and other public or semi-public agents have launched policies of social and economic development, i.e. the promotion of SMEs, job creation, etc., to combat inefficient organization and management problems or housing quality and shortages. However, the consecutive policies implemented in the 1970s and 1980s in this locality have proved insufficient to defeat a twofold pattern: a process of suburbanization and an inner city trend leading to the concentration of an economically weak population with a large number of migrants. The major obstacle for the formulation and implementation of an effective urban development policy in Hamburg is the particular institutional structure, since Hamburg nearly coincides territorially with the *Land* Hamburg. Thus, due to the subordinate taxation basis, a significant part of the wealthiest strata have moved to the adjoining states of Schleswig-Holstein and Lower Saxony. This has affected all urban redevelopment and an economic restructuring policy promoted by local authorities and has made the Hamburg *Land* economically dependent upon the adjoining states. However, Hamburg has been quite strong about an alternative policy agenda and is taking the weakness and/or the adverse effects produced by the institutionalization of policies to counteract economic and social recession into account.

Barakaldo's case highlights the complex institutional jungle at the heart of local initiatives. Economic restructuring initiatives are undertaken by the local, provincial, regional, and central administrations. The different administrative levels co-operate and compete with diverse initiatives and policies both at the local and supra-local levels. For example, the Basque government has designed a series of programmes to improve economic competitiveness by promoting inter-firm co-operation schemes in specific areas such as technological innovation and development, creation of commercial networks, foreign trade, etc.

The six cities analysed here present a picture of comparable and still quite uneven development paths. All of them except for Antwerp and Girona show a considerable loss or a stagnation in employment over the last twenty to twenty-five years. Charleroi, Bilbao, and Rostock are struggling to find their way out of a manufacturing crisis that cost them half their manufacturing employment, and left them with old capital stock and quite rigid institutions, either due to a long history of Fordist public intervention, capitalist conservatism, or socialist central planning. The imprint of a heavy industry business culture and the low levels of economic diversification contribute to their relatively low dynamism compared to other localities in our sample. The increasing role of local actors, institutions, and public/private networks to cope with unemployment and restructuring dynamics appears to be one of the key factors in strengthening socio-economic cohesion. Indeed, new innovative initiatives in these localities are highly dependent on selective institutional innovation.

Hamburg, Antwerp, and Girona are also pursuing institutional innovation. Both Antwerp and Hamburg are quite prosperous harbour cities, accomplishing high growth scores. But Hamburg's growth is jobless, whereas Antwerp's is insufficient to match labour supply. The traditional entente between harbour capital and city hall today seems incapable of creating new jobs and incomes for all citizens. The global harbours which until recently followed a 'city marketing' approach to strengthen their economy, are caught in the NEP spiral, but are trying to escape it through initiatives in the social economy. Cooperation with civil society and the European Union is very important in this respect.

5.3. Innovative initiatives for alternative integrated strategies

Taking into account the specific development trajectories of localities, their basic needs, and development potential, we now investigate how Integrated Area Development initiatives can overcome a strictly physical and economist orientation of local development, and include social priorities and social policy objectives. Several innovative initiatives in urban development are presented for our six case-study cities.

In each case there is a stronger or weaker will to produce an alternative policy agenda that attempts to integrate the needs of deprived population strata into the development strategies. In Chapter 4 we provided an overview of different dimensions of the Integrated Area Development approach and pointed out how only a few localities or neighbourhoods managed to combine all dimensions of social innovation in local development. Still these experiences are quite encouraging and worth a detailed scrutiny. The various dimensions of social innovation in development practice can be classified in terms of alternative strategies:

(*a*) Actions in favour of, and based on, the mobilization of the local population and the build-up of a local 'conscience';

(*b*) Actions reinforcing links between economic strategies and social policies;

(*c*) Vocational training adapted to the needs and the capabilities of the local population;

(*d*) Actions developing production activities, meeting local needs, with potential new jobs for local people.

In this chapter, this classification, representing different foci of the Integrated Area Development model, will serve as a guideline for the presentation of the different experiences in local development.

5.3.1. North-east Antwerp

The start of integrated local development actions in north-east Antwerp should be situated in the complex web of actors and initiatives that have developed since the beginning of the 1990s. Two periods can be distinguished: 1990–4 in which an intuitive strategy for urban neighbourhood development in Antwerp was designed, and 1995 till today when the city together with the other actors designed a neighbourhood development plan and when the neighbourhood of north-east Antwerp became part of the URBAN programme. The main actor in the whole process is the BOM (Buurtontwikkelingsmaatschappij; or the 'Neighbourhood Development Corporation'), a network of seven actors from the public and private sector that was created to participate in the Third Poverty

Programme of the European Union. BOM mainly acts as a project developer and a facilitator of relationships between different actors, projects, and funding institutions (Nieuwinckel 1996: 237–8). Its strategy aims at multidimensional projects mostly in line with the Integrated Area Development model.

In order to present in a coherent way the various axes of local development in north-east Antwerp, we will revisit Fig. 4.1 summarizing the Integrated Area Development model, but this time filling in Antwerp labels.

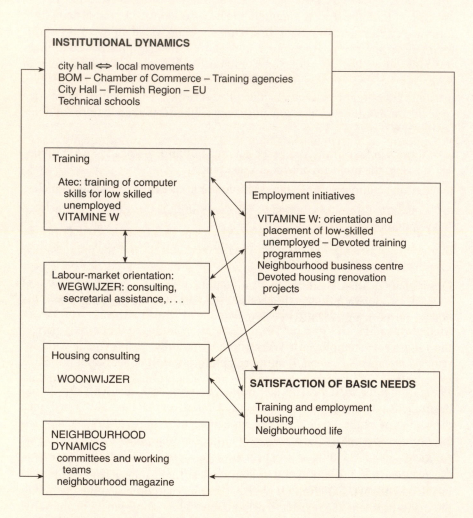

Fig. 5.1. Integrated Area Development in north-east Antwerp

Actions in favour of, and based on, the mobilization of the local population and the build-up of a local 'conscience'

Co-ordinated by BOM, in north-east Antwerp a sports hall was built by youngsters who had dropped out from school. For this project, an alternating learning–work system was developed, which led the participating technical school to change the content and form of its teaching. The registered young-sters discovered for the first time the professional world, gained confidence in their own capacities, learned about the effort needed to enter the professional world, and also received a small salary. This sports hall also met a basic need in this neighbourhood of 35,000 inhabitants, where not a single public hall was accessible to young people. The hall is run by a variety of youth associations, which should help youngsters become aware of their responsibilities and over-come ethnic barriers.

BOM has also contributed to the launching of a quarterly neighbourhood magazine by various associations of the neighbourhood. This magazine is written and composed by neighbourhood inhabitants and distributed free (22,000 copies) to all mailboxes in the neighbourhood. It is partly funded through advertising.

The socio-cultural dimension of BOM actions is very important and plays a part in the economic initiative and the housing actions spurred on by BOM. Since unemployment and poor housing quality are perceived as the main prob-lems of the neighbourhoods, most actions are meant to overcome them.

Actions reinforcing links between economic strategies and social policies

Within this domain, two important BOM actions should be cited: the opening of a centre of orientation for job seekers (Werkwijzer) and the creation of a support structure for the renovation of houses by their occupants (Woonwijzer).

Werkwijzer was created by BOM in collaboration with the VDAB (Vlaamse Dienst voor Arbeidsbemiddeling, i.e. the Flemish Service for Work Mediation) and with Vitamine W (an association aiming at the employment of the long-term unemployed). Werkwijzer is the only 'employment window' (*guichet unique pour l'emploi*) in the neighbourhood. It collects and publishes job openings, offers personal consulting and orientation to job seekers in their job-search trajectory. It also provides material services to jobseekers (type-writers or word-processing, photocopying, etc).

The creation of Werkwijzer can be considered as successful, because a specific population has been reached. Another Werkwijzer was opened by BOM in another neighbourhood of Antwerp. And the VDAB learned from the experience by decentralizing its own services to the long-term unemployed to the neighbourhood level. Of course, these services do not solve the unem-ployment problem: the registered persons have a low employment probability, because of their low training level, their lack of work experience, and their unrelatedness to the socio-economic domain. Therefore, BOM is working on adapted training programmes, influencing the demand side of the labour-market, by making the entrepreneurs of the Antwerp agglomeration sensitive to the issue.

Woonwijzer can be considered as a housing improvement consulting office. It is the locus of information and advice for the neighbourhood inhabitants with respect to housing renovation. One of the missions of Woonwijzer is to diffuse information on the public subsidies for renovation. Woonwijzer helps the candidates for subsidies to complete the application forms and to deal with the administration.

Woonwijzer also provides technical knowledge for the formulation of the individual renovation plans, including an estimate of cost. It lends equipment and tools, including scaffolding that can be delivered and assembled on the spot.

Vocational training adapted to the needs and the capabilities of the population

In April 1991, BOM established ATec, a training centre for modern technologies (computing and office automation). By setting up training initiatives for people with a low schooling level, the long-term unemployed, and beneficiaries of the minimum income, ATec differs from other training bodies in Antwerp, which impose rather strict criteria on the candidates for traineeships. This is the case with the VDAB, the body for the placement of unemployed that utilizes formalized and rigid training procedures. ATec does not seek to expand its activities to other segments of the labour-market.

The main training programme offered by ATec is for computer technicians. It lasts five months and includes a work experience of five weeks. The learning process is very concrete and experience oriented. The trainees must solve practical problems regarding the installation, maintenance, and repair of computers and networks. From the outset, the objective 'labour-market integration' was attained. Among the fifty-seven persons who followed one of the first three traineeships, forty-two found a job during or at the end of it (or 73 per cent). It is important to stress that these people did not reply to published job openings, but were placed through informal contacts. ATec has clearly developed relations of trust with several enterprises in the Antwerp region.

Actions developing production activities, meeting local needs, with potential new jobs for the local population

BOM also supported the creation of a business centre in the neighbourhood. This complex project went through different stages and only became operational in 1996.

In the beginning the project favoured the creation of economic activities by residents of the neighbourhood, more specifically the unemployed. But because of the uncertainty surrounding many social economy projects, BOM gradually began to orient itself towards the competitive economic sector. For a while the idea to select projects that would have a direct effect on the neighbourhood was fostered: renovation of buildings, or services that could be entrusted to persons seeking reinsertion into the labour-market. This presence of socio-economic objectives, even in a weakened form, was not exactly in line with the wishes of some of the partners of BOM, such as the business community and the unions. Therefore, it was decided that the business centre should function completely within the formal economy, with socio-economic activities developed elsewhere in the BOM repertoire. The implementation of the project also suffered delays because of funding problems. Big enterprises, which were approached to provide capital, pulled out for fear of profitability problems. The main funding of the enterprise centre finally came from the European Union with its Urban Pilot Project in Antwerp. But the centre should ultimately become self-sufficient.

In its new version, the centre also seeks to attract start-up SMEs to the neighbourhood, in particular in four sectors: administrative services, professional services, artisan production, and distribution. Small working spaces can be rented at limited rates and meeting rooms are available. About thirty firms can be housed. The centre also offers the traditional cocktail of professional services: management, accounting, secretarial support, marketing. These services are also accessible to firms which are already working in the neighbourhood. The building of the business centre—a former school—has been completely renovated. It includes a restaurant and an exhibition room, which could become a meeting place for Antwerp business people and for the local neighbourhood population.

In the case of Antwerp, a large metropolis with an economy widely open to the world and to global forces, it is interesting to see that a relatively undercapitalized strategy of integrated development at a neighbourhood level was feasible. This strategy has already produced significant results in terms of the professional integration of unemployment, renewal of housing, economic regeneration, and institutional innovation. In these four domains, these different projects are complementary to the orthodox strategies established at higher spatial scales, but which have a weak positive, and often a negative impact, on the economic and social dynamics of the neighbourhood.

At the same time, the strategy of BOM constitutes, by its multidimensional and integrated character, an alternative to many urban strategies. The observation period, now close to ten years, is too short to be able to grasp all aspects, but today in Belgium BOM is recognized as a model of bottom-up and decentralized integrated action. Other institutions of the same type are being established in other neighbourhoods of Antwerp and in other Flemish cities, for example Ghent.

5.3.2. Hamburg

In Hamburg the city and the state were bound to search for an alternative strategy taking into consideration the jobless growth in both main sectors

Table 5.4. *The main initiatives of BOM since 1990*

Main achievements
Centre for counselling job searchers (Werkwijzer) Training centre for new technologies (ATec) NOA Business Centre
Advice centre for the renovation of private dwellings (Woonwijzer) Refurbishing of housing blocks, combined with the renovation of public space and social involvement Renovation of social housing lots, enabling the rehousing of unemployed and socially excluded people
Building of a sports hall, by and for the youngsters of the district District newspaper (22,000 copies), written by inhabitants, with costs partially covered by advertising Annual guide of social and cultural organizations of the district

(manufacturing and services) combined and the adverse effects produced by the 'official' programmes. Initiatives were taken which cut through the entire policy system, such as the Hamburg Economic Development Corporation established in 1985 to provide consultancy services for firms locating in Hamburg. Since 1994 the city has attempted to co-ordinate its anti-poverty policy within a framework concept (see below), while other initiatives and actions of more specific sectoral and geographic objectives were also undertaken.

Actions in favour of, and based on, the mobilization of the local population and the build-up of a local 'conscience'

The uniqueness of Hamburg in the German context is highlighted by the mere fact that public action has institutionalized its will to act positively in the field of employment generation and local development, based on a close collaboration with non-governmental institutions. It would seem that in Hamburg the trend towards mobilization of the localities and the building up of a local 'conscience' dates from the early 1980s, with actions promoted by the *Netzwerk* organization. These have been focusing on forging links between the private sector and the local authorities. In this climate creative local civil institutions, among them the Johann Daniel Lawaetz-Stiftung, have become quite effective.

Actions reinforcing links between economic strategies and social policies

An integration of the struggle against poverty, unemployment, and housing shortage based on the empowerment of the affected populations in deprived neighbourhoods—the official policy of Hamburg city—has led to remarkable results. The example of the Lawaetz Stiftung is quite convincing in this respect.

The Lawaetz Stiftung was created in 1986.[2] In 1987 it was recognized as an alternative development agency (AST). The Foundation seldom becomes involved in carrying out projects, but develops, co-ordinates, or advises them, and provides training and research on local development issues (see Fig. 5.2). Accomplished actions range from 'self-help' and communal living projects to neighbourhood-bound socio-economic activities. The housing projects are usually subsidized through the alternative construction management scheme (ABB programme). Future tenants are also involved in the building work

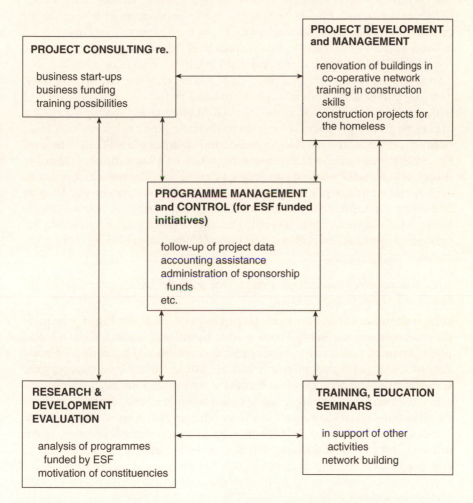

PROJECT CONSULTING re.

business start-ups
business funding
training possibilities

PROJECT DEVELOPMENT and MANAGEMENT

renovation of buildings in
   co-operative network
training in construction
   skills
construction projects for
   the homeless

PROGRAMME MANAGEMENT and CONTROL (for ESF funded initiatives)

follow-up of project data
accounting assistance
administration of sponsorship
   funds
etc.

RESEARCH & DEVELOPMENT EVALUATION

analysis of programmes
   funded by ESF
motivation of constituencies

TRAINING, EDUCATION SEMINARS

in support of other
   activities
network building

Fig. 5.2. Activity domains of the Johan Daniel Lawaetz-Stiftung

[2] The name goes back to the enlighted industrialist Johann Daniel Lawaetz (1750–1826) who was involved in the struggle against poverty during the industrial revolution. He especially promoted self-help initiatives.

themselves. In recent years the Foundation has also played an important role in consulting and mediating with regard to the European Social Fund.

Vocational training adapted to the needs and the capabilities of the population

Since the early 1980s, in order to deal with problems emerging from structural weaknesses of the labour-market (lack of specialized labour) and the relative absence of transmission mechanisms between big firms and SMEs, a variety of initiatives for the creation of supporting institutions both in the public, the non-governmental, and the private sector were taken. BAGS, for instance (Behörde der Arbeit, Gesundheit und Soziales: Department of Work, Health and Social Welfare), has founded a number of non-governmental institutions in order to deal with a variety of social problems. The core of such institutions has been ZEBRA (Centre for Vocational Training) which in turn has been co-operating with others such as: Arbeit und Lernen Hamburg GmbH (Working and Learning, a non-profit institution founded by the Unions and the AWO with the purpose to provide jobs for unskilled labour). Moreover, experience in Hamburg in employment generation has been marked by the creation of two public institutions: the Hamburger Arbeit and Hamburg-West Gmbh. In turn, by 1982, a local economic development policy had been initiated with the 'Programm Hamburger Neue Beschäftigungspolitik'. The welfare segment of such programmes has gradually focused on job creation schemes, and later on education and training. Economic recession and economic cuts imposed by the Federal Government have altered again the priorities of the welfare pro-gramme giving emphasis to long-term unemployed, unskilled, handicapped, and foreign populations.

Actions developing production activities, meeting local needs, with potential new jobs for local people

One could argue that the most interesting facet of the Hamburg experience is the local competence that has been gradually built up, leading to the adapta-tion of training initiatives to local needs and capacities. The cornerstones for the building up of such ability have been initiatives tailored to housing provi-sion and maintenance. This has become a widespread culture inspiring the city's initiatives as a whole; it has been extended and even more formalized with the 'AST–ABB' concept (an urban renewal philosophy which incorp-orates the participation of problem labour groups in the building and design process). This concept has in consequence been applied to other fields of action, related to the employment and production needs of more advanced sec-tors (e.g. ecological technology through the activities of *Ökologische Technik e. V* (ecological technology).

   In conclusion, it is important to stress the local awareness of the limits and effects of 'formal' policies developed through 'official' institutional routes; and, in parallel, the inherent attempt to produce alternative policies integrat-ing social issues (combining for instance planning, housing, and employment policy). The 'unifying force' of all these are citizens' initiatives and self-help actions.

Second, the impressive thing about Hamburg lies in the mere fact that most official local Authority and *Land* institutions (and even those of the central state) present a unique capacity to co-operate amongst themselves and with non-governmental institutions, and systematically to involve the private sector in such activities and to integrate the social component in most of these joint actions. Apparently, Hamburg proves to be close to what can be defined as a successful local integrated action. This is also strongly reflected in the *Programm Armutsbekämpfung* launched by the city of Hamburg's Senate in 1994 as a framework (*Rahmenkonzept*) for various integrated actions in the struggle against poverty. This concept is in line with the Integrated Area Development policy put forward in this book. It focuses on housing and working in urban neighbourhoods, by promoting integrated actions. In this way, the Senate wants to recognize that both housing and work are of basic existential value for the inhabitants in these areas. Economic activities and financial viable housing must be geared towards the needs of the inhabitants. The latter must be involved in decision-making processes, in concrete initiatives, and in the evaluation of the results. Intermediate structures co-ordinate the various actions in the eight pilot neighbourhoods, but they remain at all times under democratic control. Projects must be based on partnership and bottom-up initiatives, preferably coming from the concerned urban groups (Freie und Hansestadt Hamburg 1994). Of course, even if this framework mainly remains an organizational device, several of the projects that have been accomplished in the inner city of Hamburg show its operational value.

Table 5.5. *Innovative institutions, actions, and programmes in Hamburg*

Main innovations
Hamburger Arbeit, 1983
Hamburg-West GmbH, 1988
Programm Hamburger Neue Beschäftigungspolitik
Netzwerk Organisation
Johann Daniel Lawaetz-Stiftung, created in 1986
AST-ABB Concept, 1986/84
ZEBRA (Centre for Vocational Training)
Arbeit und Lernen Hamburg GmbH, non-profit institution
Programm Armutsbekämpfung, 1994
Ökologische Technik e.V

Source: Häussermann *et al.*; 1993*a*, 1993*b*; Lawaetz Stiftung

5.3.3. Barakaldo (Bilbao)

In Barakaldo, innovative initiatives for alternative strategies are closely related to the participation of this municipality in the European Union programme 'Neighbourhoods in Crisis'[3]. This programme was intended to create a network of European cities committed to the rehabilitation of declining urban centres by means of an integrated development approach. This implied not only multidimensional actions, but also co-ordination among the political, technical, and social actors of the area. In official language, the main objectives of this programme were to stimulate the application of all the potential capabilities of local actors and support a permanent dialogue among them; to introduce a more global perspective to the area's problems; to support the development of entities to act at the local level; to take advantage of the synergies of public and private financing; and to promote a radical change of image of the neighbourhood (Rontegi). Barakaldo joined this network in November 1991.

One of the first actions related to Barakaldo's participation in the 'Neighbourhoods in Crisis' network was to set up a local agency, Inguralde, integrating the different actors involved in the community. Inguralde was defined as the 'Institution for the Integral Development of Barakaldo', in charge of managing the project. The first phase of the project involved the exchange of experiences among the participating cities. During the following phase (1992–4) Inguralde set up a series of initiatives and programmes oriented towards the rehabilitation of the neighbourhood. These included an information and consciousness-raising campaign on health and the environment, cultural exchanges, training courses, physical renewal initiatives, field work on the area, workshop schools, etc.

However, by 1995, Inguralde had entered a new phase, narrowing its field of action to two areas: the promotion of employment initiatives and occupational training. And, by 1996, this move was followed by the extension of its area of intervention from a single neighbourhood (Rontegi) to the whole municipality (Barakaldo). After a radical change of its organic structure, the agency changed its name to the Inguralde-Municipal Autonomous Body for the Development of Barakaldo. This change reflected its reconversion into a 'municipal service centre for occupational training, employment, and economic promotion'.

Today, Inguralde's intervention is concentrated in five areas:

- training: occupational, continuing education, practical training in firms, and employment training;
- employment orientation and labour-market integration: job market information, motivation and personalized orientation, traineeships;
- economic promotion: information, technical assistance, and training for existing firms;
- retailing promotion: technical assistance, training, dynamizing, and promotion of retailing activity;

---

[3] This network still exists and Barakaldo has an active presence through Inguralde, the local development agency.

- self-employment: information and orientation, seminars, and courses for the creation of new firms and firm incubator.

Actions in favour of, and based on, the mobilization of the local people and the build-up of a local 'conscience'

Most of the actions related to the mobilization of local residents were conceived and implemented during the first phase of the establishment of Inguralde. The recognition that a strategy of integrated development was necessarily tied to greater involvement of the local population, was a fundamental idea behind the 'Neighbourhoods in Crisis' programme. Thus, the emphasis on citizens' participation was a constituent element of both the organic structure of Inguralde, as well as of its operating dynamics.

The creation of a *Patronato* made up of city council members representing all political parties, a representative of the county level government (*Diputación*), and a representative of the Employment Institute (central administration level) was complemented with the participation of four representatives from local groups and one elected member from the neighbourhood association. At the same time, five 'working groups' were also set up to channel citizens' participation in the definition and implementation of the integrated development strategy. The role of the working groups was critical. They were made up of representatives from neighbourhood associations as well as representatives from the city council, and members of the technical staff of the agency. These committees were asked to discuss and advance proposals of action for the area which would then be evaluated by the city council for approval or refusal. The five working groups (culture, health care, social welfare, urbanism, and employment and local development) addressed those fields of intervention considered as most problematic in the area. The idea was that this mode of operation would allow for an increasing role for local citizens in municipal policy-making processes.

However, since 1995, changes in the scope and functions of Inguralde have been followed by a gradual move towards a more technocratic approach in the operation of the agency. This meant, in particular, the suppression of the *Patronato* and the 'working groups' in 1995 as the agency reorganized and extended its field of intervention to the whole municipality. Despite the removal of institutionalized mechanisms for citizen participation within Inguralde, however, the initial philosophy remained present in such programmes as a consciousness-raising campaign about the problems of Rontegi and the work of Inguralde (1993), and a campaign to raise local consciousness on civic participation in the neighbourhood.

Actions reinforcing links between economic strategies and social policies

In Barakaldo, recognition of the need for an integrated development strategy has led to a focus on the least favoured sectors of the society. Indeed, one of the specific objectives of Inguralde is to 'facilitate social and labour market integration of the most marginalised social groups' (Annual Report 1995).

As part of the activities related to vocational training, Inguralde manages part of the URBAN-Barakaldo programme, financed through the European Commission Structural Funds for the period 1994–9. This programme incorporates the experience of the 'Neighbourhoods in Crisis' project, focusing on integrated actions within those neighbourhoods but the site of intervention is different from the one selected for the 'Neighbourhoods in Crisis' project. The URBAN-Barakaldo plan comprises the whole urban area of Barakaldo but a more specific one, the URBAN-Galindo programme, singles out a derelict area of over 50 ha. located between the urban centre and the river, left abandoned after the closure of the steel mills.

The objective of the URBAN-Barakaldo plan is to develop an integrated programme by means of complementary urban renewal, environmental, social, and occupational training initiatives to promote local economic development, to combat social and labour market exclusion, and to reduce the levels of uncertainty and vulnerability of local residents.

The URBAN-Galindo operation focuses on a particular area. From an urban planning point of view, it involves the construction of a new plaza, green areas (12.5 ha.), urbanization of some streets and plazas, and a connection to the old docks as well as the construction of 2,000 new housing units (16 ha.). From an economic perspective, the plan includes extensive land reclamation of contaminated soil, revitalization of retailing activities, and the creation of a Centre for the development of small and medium-sized companies in an area of approximately 4.1 ha. The social dimension involves the promotion of a series of social programmes for infants, families, and the elderly as well as occupational training and labour-market insertion initiatives. Leisure infrastructure and an environmental thematic park (4.8 ha.) are also included among the initiatives. The estimated investment amounts to 3,200 million ptas, co-financed by the European Union and the local administrations. The operation is managed by Bilbao Ría 2000, a semi-public urban development corporation set up to guide and manage the revitalization of the whole metropolitan area. The role of Inguralde is to establish and develop the occupational training actions envisaged in the URBAN programme. Since 1997, unemployed groups with low qualification levels have participated in two training programmes: one on housing rehabilitation (364 hours) and one on domestic repair and maintenance tasks (250 hours). Other shorter courses include urban waste management, installation of TV and video antennas, and a course on industrial cleaning.

Vocational training adapted to the needs and the capabilities of the population

Since the reorganization of Inguralde in 1995, occupational training has been one of the key fields of intervention of the agency. The initiatives have developed along two axes:

(*a*) the development of vocational training programmes for the least qualified sectors of society and those with the greatest difficulty in accessing the job market such as the long-term unemployed. These programmes are developed in co-ordination with the social welfare department of the city council and with local groups organized to counter unemployment;

(*b*) initiatives related to the development of the URBAN-Barakaldo programme where Inguralde co-ordinates the occupational training schemes designed for the Galindo area. In this way, the agency has set up a series of training courses on physical renewal, housing rehabilitation, and environmental recovery. Several public buildings are being renewed under this scheme.

Besides, since 1994, Inguralde has launched a number of training programmes. Between 1995 and 1997 more than 1,100 students have followed these courses with an investment of approximately 700 million ptas. The funds come from the various levels of public administration: the municipality, the Diputación, the Basque government, and the European Union.

Finally, a complementary area of intervention involves labour-market orientation and insertion: labour-market information, motivation, and personalized orientation, traineeships, etc. A self-employment orientation programme has also been established to provide the necessary training for new 'entrepreneurs'.

Actions developing production activities, meeting local needs, with potential new jobs for the local population

Three types of initiatives oriented to the development of new productive activities meeting local needs can be distinguished: consulting for existing SMEs, promotion of retail trade, and encouraging self-employment. In 1997, this programme supported fifteen new projects with more than forty new jobs created.

Since 1995, Inguralde has gradually evolved into a self-defined 'municipal service centre for occupational training, employment and economic promotion' operating at the level of the whole municipality. The agency's activities are centred around five basic intervention areas: occupational training, labour-market orientation and insertion, promotion of new enterprises, commercial development, and self-employment. The enlargement of Inguralde's action radius beyond the initial neighbourhood defined for the 'Neighbourhoods in Crisis' programme is a positive step to the extent that it makes the whole municipality into an area subject to socio-economic revitalization initiatives. None the less, despite the initial co-ordinating role of the agency, Inguralde remains only one among a myriad of institutions intervening in the municipality. Dispersion, lack of co-ordination, and duplication are the consequence of this multiplicity.

Table 5.6. *Innovative actions in Barakaldo (Bilbao)*

Main innovations
Creation of working committees to channel citizens' participation in socio-economic planning and implementation
Consciousness-raising campaigns on the neighbourhood's problems to animate civic participation
Creation of a Crafts Centre for social services providing basic training for domestic care to local unemployed
Strong involvement in training initiatives within the URBAN Programme to combat unemployment and marginalization
Development of vocational training programmes for long-term unemployed
Labour-market information and orientation programmes
Initiatives to strengthen retailing activities and self-employment

5.3.4. Charleroi

Over the last fifteen years, the Public Centre for Social Action of Charleroi (CPAS) has constantly tried to reorganize its departments, to collaborate more and more with other social actors, to open up to the economic world, and to work with excluded citizens on their social and/or professional integration. From 1985 to 1989, the CPAS of Charleroi took part in the Second European Programme against Poverty, with an initiative directed towards young unemployed. Moreover, after the hard winter of 1985, during which the flaws of 'ordinary' social aid had become flagrant, several social institutions felt the need to form a partnership.[4] In 1987, they published a programme demanding 'More Solidarity, Less Poverty'. This text proposed changes in the law, but also expressed hypotheses about the fight against poverty, and called for new initiatives.

Two years later, this partnership worked out a local initiative against poverty and put it before the European Commission. This model action named 'Let's win with the losers' was subsidized by Poverty III from 1990 to 1994. More than sixty local institutions became involved in one of the projects. The focus lay with initiatives regarding training or social reintegration and housing.

Local initiatives for training and integration

From 1981 to 1988, the number of people depending on the Public Centre for Social Aid (CPAS) for their subsistence income doubled. The proportion of young people living on the minimum income increased from 29.5 per cent in 1976 to 41.4 per cent ten years later. The support provided by the minimum

---

[4] These institutions are: the CPAS of Charleroi, ATD Quart Monde, La Ligue des Familles, the Union des Villes et Communes Belges, and two popular education organizations, one socialist—Présence et Action Culturelles, and the other one Catholic—the Mouvement Ouvrier Chrétien.

income may easily produce a condition of 'assistance' especially since in Belgium young people have a right to the minimum income and also since this measure is not accompanied by insertion into the work process or training. It is significant that 30 per cent of the people living on the minimum income for more than two years are less than 30 years old. The CPAS of Charleroi soon became aware of this problem. It began then, like other CPASs in Wallonia, a move towards training and concrete work situations, in order to bypass the beaten tracks of aid and assistance. This move is all the more difficult because the people concerned, or their families, have suffered from social problems (juvenile delinquency, conjugal problems, alcoholism, drug addiction), which have kept them in 'risk groups'. For these people, the CPAS has, since 1978, developed various actions. The sums laid out grew from 0.5 million Belgian francs in 1978 to 40 million francs in 1994.

At the moment, the CPAS is working in three directions: remotivation; resocializing and on-the-job training; the promotion of access to a qualified job.

Renewing the motivation of the young unemployed, and, more generally, of the people supported by the CPAS, was, at the beginning, carried out in a quite traditional way by social workers, belonging to the CPAS or to NGOs. But this type of action has some limitations: very quickly, aid becomes assistance and it gets very difficult to escape this trap (Bodson and Hiernaux 1981). On the other hand, the growing number of people depending on the CPAS was threatening the smooth operation of the system. This is why the CPAS of Charleroi has redeployed its services, and established partnerships with other local institutions. Passage 45 was established. It is a unique social reception office, where people normally working in different institutions (all funded by the CPAS) collaborate. This principle of mixing different institutions is highly justified, since, as the manager of Passage 45 notes, 'the initial request of the people who come here is just to have access to a service desk'. Besides receiving people, each institution keeps its own mission (to advise the youngsters on their rights, to help children with their homework, to propose a training action, etc.) But, by working through Passage 45, each institution is led to adopt *vis-à-vis* the persons received, a multidimensional approach. Fully adapted answers and advice are delivered.

From 1985 to 1989, within the framework of the second EC programme to combat poverty, the CPAS of Charleroi set up several *chantiers-formation* (training actions on working sites). These are, in a way, intermediary firms, offering to young people the possibility to work. The youngsters who were hired had a low skill level. Within these production units, the daily work contributed to broadening their knowledge, their abilities, their professional and technical know-how, but also their 'know-be'. These devices for resocializing proved their value and some of them are still running.

To help the young unemployed to find qualified jobs, various local institutions were created in 1991, within the framework of Poverty III, by the Regional Mission for Employment in Charleroi (Mirec). These projects were inspired explicitly by the action in France of Bertrand Schwartz. Mirec is similar to a French *mission locale*, since it has a multidimensional approach. An offer of a job or a training course to a youngster is always accompanied by the chance to work on his or her social and psychological problems. Mirec does not pick people on the basis of scholarly criteria, but rather by evaluating their health, their motivation, and their ability to learn.

All these various initiatives induce a more intensive collaboration among institutions which, traditionally, dealt either with social aid, or with employment and training, but never with both. The projects show a constant determination to help the least privileged groups to carve out a place in society. From this point of view, a development action from below has a great advantage over policies from above: perverse effects (such as the selection of target groups, estranging of institutions from the real world, etc.) still exist, but they are more easily overcome. A gradual opening up towards the business world is also a favourable aspect.

The most obvious limit to these various plans is the relatively small number of young people involved. For instance, the *chantiers-formation* received, from 1986 to 1990, 543 young people, that is 19 per cent of the youngsters eligible for the minimum income. But, due to the seriousness of the social disintegration of Charleroi, it is not surprising that the local initiatives for social insertion and training have more qualitative than quantitative aims.

Local initiatives in the field of housing

The *Fonds du Logement des Familles Nombreuses* (FLFN) and the *Interrégionale Wallonne des Habitants de Cité* (IWHC) led a first initiative. The former institution is a social housing society, the latter was founded as a tenants' organization, in order to intervene in the procedures for allocating housing. It then extended its actions to a certain number of the problems experienced by tenants. Nowadays, in Charleroi, some families find themselves at the end of an impoverishment process, in a state of chronic eviction. The level of indebtedness is so high that working no longer means very much. In these cases providing another dwelling is not sufficient; in order to help these families to reintegrate themselves into normal social dynamics, they must be accompanied step by step. The FLFN experimentally provided a dwelling to one of these families, in return for a convention signed by the 'tenant' and an agreement from the IWHC to aid this family. The family was pushed to pay the rent, to look for a job, to look for a stable dwelling, etc. The experiment was successful and is regularly repeated. It contrasts with traditional social aid to families, which is punctual, distant from them, and continued over long periods of time.

The second initiative, led by the CPAS, aimed to enlarge the access of people living on the minimum income to social housing. The CPAS sought to establish an agreement on housing quotas for these people with every social housing society. The answers were not very favourable, since only forty flats were finally involved. Moreover, it is thought that some housing corporations may have substituted some less privileged households for others, in order to enjoy certain advantages provided by the agreement. Therefore the results of the experiment are hard to evaluate.

The actions launched during the last fifteen years (first within the Poverty II programme, then within Poverty III, now within URBAN) aimed at tackling the very serious social problems that result from the economic disintegration of the locality. Since the early 1970s, the increase in the number of unemployed people has been strong and cumulative. More than 20 per cent of the local population experiences poverty and exclusion. Thus, the seriousness of the situation has led various local institutions to put their differences aside and to collaborate. The many actions that were launched in the social field valorize this partnership. Due to the difficult social situation, actions for the least privileged groups have been put at the top of the agenda. But it should be stressed that these actions can hardly, on their own, lay the foundations of an Integrated Area Development of Charleroi. At this stage, two main criticisms should be made.

First, the set of initiatives carried out by the CPAS and its partners lack a territorial dimension. The territory of Charleroi is geographically sprawling (measuring more than 100 sq. km.), socially heterogeneous, and historically fragmented. Moreover, whereas neighbourhood social relations are crucial for the reintegration of unemployed and/or socially excluded people, very few initiatives are carried out at that level, for equity as well as practical reasons.

In recent years, the municipality of Charleroi has become aware of a need to create urban districts with a human scale within its boundaries. In 1995, it instituted fifty-five districts, each being the locus of social services provision and of so-called 'renewed local democracy'. A new municipal service is in charge of implementing this approach. This Service de Développement des Quartiers has three main tasks: (i) to take into account the expectations of the inhabitants with regard to the physical upgrading of their district; (ii) to promote a social animation at the neighbourhood level. This includes the participation of volunteers and of not-for-profit organizations in education and culture; (iii) to create a statistical data base supporting the decision-making and the policy evaluation process.

Second, very few local initiatives to combat poverty induce collaboration with firms and/or economic institutions. There seem to be few links between the actions which we studied and local projects of economic development. This gap between economic promotion and social action is worrying and has led to a misallocation of resources. For instance, over the period 1975–90, 90 per cent of the ERDF funds allocated to Charleroi were devoted to the development of large infrastructures. But the effects of these investments are not convincing (Van Doren 1996). It should be mentioned, however, that a significant part of the local population mistrusts the initiatives to regenerate the local economy.

For these people, the economic initiatives follow a logic of profit and competitiveness—i.e. values which have not been 'incorporated' or have been rejected by the alienated population. This may explain why the socialist municipality of Charleroi is not keen on establishing bridges between the fight against social exclusion and economic development strategies.

Table 5.7. *The main socio-economic initiatives in Charleroi since 1990*

Main innovations

Centre for consulting for young job searchers (Mirec)
Chantiers-Formation (work training experiences)

Guidance scheme for low-income tenants
Refurbishing of housing lots, enabling the reinsertion of unemployed and socially excluded
  people
Production of guide of social and cultural organizations in the urban region

Creation of 55 urban districts providing social services and fostering local democracy

Creation of a data base in the fields of housing, social services, and employment supporting the
  decision-making and policy evaluation process

5.3.5. Rostock

In Rostock everything seems in the phase of 'being created' (the market, the local state, etc.). Under such transitional circumstances the locality cannot be examined with the same analytical rationale as the case studies already considered.

Actions in favour of, and based on, the mobilization of the local population and the build-up of a local 'conscience'

In line with the socialist past, till 1993, the central state and the *Land* (region) primarily promoted the development agenda. This top-down approach has partly contributed to the building up of a local 'conscience' in a city with a limited tradition of civil society and private enterprise. There is, however, a growing potential for local mobilization and 'conscience' building, as manifested by the growing number of non-governmental institutions and by the consolidation of local 'conventional institutions and policies'.

Actions reinforcing links between economic strategies and social policies

Set in this transitional context, all policy actions tend to assume an exceptional status, either through the adoption of federal programmes (especially designed for former East Germany areas e.g. 'Aufschwung Ost'), or through the adjustment of federal institutions to meet local needs (e.g. Federal Employment Office).

Vocational training adapted to the needs and the capabilities of the population

The city of Rostock and other institutions also established *Beschäftigungs- und Qualifizierungsgesellschaften* (BQGs or employment and training associations), an institutional innovation stemming from West German cities. They are staffed with people who advise workers on retraining and re-employment options, often opening the way to ABM (*Arbeitsbeschaffungsmassnahmen*) or jobs created in the public or non-profit sector. In Rostock BQGs have existed in all major industries. They were prominent in the shipbuilding sector; fifteen associations were linked with DMS, the shipbuilding conglomerate, and organized into an umbrella organization known as Trägergesellschaft Schiffbau (TGS) (Häussermann *et al.* 1993*b*). In 1993 these TGS associations included 5,500 workers; today they have practically faded away.

Actions developing production activities, meeting local needs, with potential new jobs for local people

Since 1991 housing renovation and construction has been adopted as a means for integrating economic strategies serving specific target groups in the urban planning approach. Within this policy context various initiatives have been launched for the restoration of parts of the town hall, the reconstruction of Rostock's water tower, the repair of the Petric church foundation, etc. These have been the outcome of activities developed by a private not-for-profit association Arche which has expanded its field of operation to low-cost housing renewal (Schubert 1995). Since 1996, the city of Rostock has been involved in an Urban Programme covering a small part of the Kröpeliner-Tor-Vorstadt (see section 5.2). This EU URBAN programme, combining urban renovation, and local economy and ecological initiatives, plays a catalysing role in changing the city's exogenous city planning approach (the post-Treuhandanstalt syndrome?) into an endogenous city-marketing approach (Schubert 1995, 1998).[5] A real problem with this URBAN project is that its 30 million DM is concentrated on an area of only 41 ha. As a consequence, many social projects move from elsewhere in the city to the URBAN area. Another negative aspect is that social housing is not a priority in this URBAN operation and the gentrification process has made many low-income and large households move out. But, despite these shortcomings, the city planners in Rostock evaluate the URBAN project as positive. It opened out for them a whole new world of multidimensional and integrated planning approaches until recently unknown. And there are constructive lessons to be drawn for the future. The closer collaboration between the city, the *Land*, and the *Bund* can offer new opportunities better to fine-tune initiatives in the field of urban renovation and (socio)-economic development. In fact the *Bund* (central state) has prepared a

---

[5] The *Land* Mecklenburg/Vorpommen has recently installed a 'Well-being Oriented Employment Project' ('Gemeinwohlorientierte Arbeitsförderprojekte') in Rostock. We do not report on this initiative in this book.

Rostock: towards an endogenous city-marketing approach?

The original (early 1990s) outlook towards spatial planning based on eradicating existing downgraded areas (e.g. Neptunwerft) and attracting external capital, has shown significant failures: increasing unemployment, lack of interest by 'foreign' capital, absence of a local socio-economic fabric to foster business links, etc.

In 1993 the Rostocker Stadtentwicklungsprogramm, complementing the Regional Spatial Planning Scheme (1993), was designed to bundle the development plans of Rostock city. It was a strategic framework in which the city's concrete city-marketing actions were situated. The city-marketing approach became operational in 1999. However, the terminology is misleading: the marketing approach defended here is much more orientated towards the improvement of living quality and the socio-economic fabric in the city than to attracting foreign firms and investors. In fact the concept as explained by the city makes us think more of sustainable development, in which social, economic, and ecological processes are interconnected, than of 'selling the city'. Large-scale projects are of course important to replace the run-down sections of urban infrastructure; but the links between these projects and neighbourhood development are carefully knitted together. In this respect, the project Kröpeliner Tor-Vorstadt (and the expected URBAN II project, which should cover an area four times the original 40 ha.) fits the new planning philosophy of Rostock Hansestadt quite well.

new socially oriented support programme for urban renewal called 'Soziale Stadt' ('Social City').

5.4. Local governance and the role of institutional innovation

Besides the changes occurring in the economic and social sphere, the process of transformation of administrative structures embraces a variety of institutional and policy levels and implies different possibilities, priorities, or even obstacles to local development initiatives. Local development initiatives could therefore be perceived and assessed in the context of an interplay of forces operating at various levels and which involve different performance criteria of institutions at supranational, national, regional, and local level. Thus it is important to identify areas of convergence and/or divergence in relation to the role of institutions and their impact on local structures and development trends in the various case studies.

5.4.1. Governance dynamics in three case-study cities

In our research, governance dynamics have been covered best in Hamburg, Antwerp, and Barakaldo (Bilbao). Hamburg is perhaps the best example of intense co-operation at different levels—among local authority departments, among federal, state (*Land*), and local governments, and among public, non-profit, and private agents. Local authority departments such as the Department of Youth and Vocational training (BSJB, Behörde der Schule, Jugend und Berufsbildung), the Department of Labour, Health and Social Affairs (BAGS, Behörde für Arbeit, Gesundheit und Soziales), and the City Development Office (STEB, Stadtentwicklungsbehörde) have supported jointly or independently the creation of several institutions and non-profit organizations in their effort to solve growing social problems. The main institution under their responsibility is ZEBRA (Zentrum zur beruflichen Qualifizierung, Centre for Vocational Qualification), an organization in charge of training the unemployed which co-operates with other institutions active in specific programmes of job creation. The Hamburg administration created two public employment companies, Hamburger Arbeit (HAB, Hamburg Labour) and Hamburg-West GmbH (HWB, West Hamburg Company) with the mission of addressing the problems of long-term unemployment and discrimination. These two companies directly provide jobs with interconnected firms and collaborate with special institutions like ZEBRA for education and vocational training. The city has recently revised its local development planning, giving it a much more democratic and integrated content. Intermediary institutions (such as the Lawaetz Foundation) play the role of co-ordinator between institutions at the city or regional level on the one hand, and neighbourhood initiatives on the other. Local democracy is guaranteed through various participatory procedures (see section 5.3.2).

The case of Antwerp is focused on a few deprived districts. In one of them, north-east Antwerp, a society for local development (BOM, Buurtontwikkelingsmaatschappij) was created by local institutions (city of Antwerp, Public Centre for Social Aid, the local organization of social workers, a university), regional institutions (the region of Flanders, the regional employment office), and the King Boudewijn Foundation to deal with poverty. BOM mainly co-ordinates already existing initiatives, and has set up specific projects to cover neglected development issues. BOM co-ordinates the local projects funded by the Flemish Fund for Integration of Disadvantaged Neighbourhoods (VFIK) and collaborates with the local office of the regional employment office and the Public Centre for Social Aid, and with the neighbourhood organizations and minority associations. BOM also participates as a partner organization in projects beyond the district. It has been involved in a strategic plan for the subregion of Antwerp initiated by the Chamber of Commerce; it is also a member of Interface, a new institution that has been created to foster collaboration between social organizations and business circles (Chamber of

Commerce, Flemish Association of Employers, the Association of Christian Employers).

In Barakaldo (Bilbao) the capacity to weave relations among local organizations was strongly enhanced by its participation in the European Union programme 'Neighbourhoods in Crisis' (1991). By emphasizing the need for co-ordinated action and permanent dialogue between the various political, technical, and social actors in the area, this programme favoured the emergence of a unique local development agency, Inguralde, bringing together the agents involved in community actions. Inguralde has significantly improved the co-ordinating and co-operative potential of the local, provincial, and regional public sector. Public institutions became involved in the agency, while the integration of citizens' collective organizations in the working committees has created a rare opportunity to build networks of co-operation for more effective and participatory action within the community. None the less, the recent extension of Inguralde's area of intervention from a single neighbourhood to the whole municipality and its concentration on the economic dimension of local development has diverted the initial emphasis on integrated and co-operative action. Moreover, despite the initial co-ordinating aim of the agency, Inguralde remains only one of a myriad of institutions intervening in the municipality and the effectiveness of its socio-economic action is still compromised by dispersion, lack of co-ordination, and overlapping of actors, agencies, initiatives, and projects.

5.4.2. Institutional innovation at the local level

It appears that institutional changes at the local level are open to constant adjustments. But at the same time, localities must comply with the policy principles and requirements to adjust to the conditions created by central state economic policy and control, and to search constantly for complementary resources from other state levels. However, it is clear that appropriate institutional leverages are often missing at the local level, which means that social targets usually run more easily into implementation problems than efforts to achieve more conventional economic projects. In many localities, systematic efforts are made to integrate training, employment, and investment and in some localities housing renewal strategies also become part of the planning agendas. The creation of new institutions exceeding the local domain and covering all aspects of local development policy is considered to be a solution for existing regulation and finance problems. The European Programme URBAN is playing a very significant pilot role here, not only with respect to its policy agenda, but also as far as its networking habits and subsidiarity practices are concerned. However, issues such as the new institutions' democratic control and the consequences for the future of local democracy arise as possible concerns.

Differences in the importance and in the forms of involvement of the local state in developmental initiatives can be seen as the further evolution of a long-

standing local government tradition in the provision of services and in repro-
ductive activities; in other cases, local development has been mostly based on
the ability of intercommunal co-operation and/or co-operation with higher
level institutions, with the central state, or other institutions. Quite frequently,
the local state has sought to promote local development initiatives through the
creation of new institutions and has, in its way, acted as a catalyst for new
governance dynamics.

6

Global Governance and
Social Change

If capitalism is to be restrained, it must be by a power of a magnitude and scope to match that of the capitalist engine itself. It must be on a global scale. The slogan 'think globally, act locally' is no longer appropriate. Local action within an unchanged global order of production and governance rapidly reaches its limits. It is necessary today not only to think about the global consequences of local action, but to act to change the global context of local action (Low and Gleeson 1999: 190).

The deep fallacy of thinking about restructuring since the oil crisis—the ultimate sign of the sprouting decline of the Fordist mode of regulation?—is the neo-liberal conviction that private economic activities have been oppressed by the public social sector. According to this conviction (see Chapter 2), expenditures for social security, social infrastructure, public education, and culture, entrusting economic and administrative functions to the state or the non-profit civilian sector, overregulating social protection and environmental quality, have squeezed the profit margins of private capital and thus undercut the basis for economic and social progress. Therefore, according to this view, a New Economic Policy (NEP), reducing the role of the state, creating a social and institutional environment that liberates trade from its public chains, that gives wings to market reach, and motivates economic agents to become more flexible (lending an ear to labour market signals?) is the sole hope for a socio-economic future of humanity (see Chapter 1).

In cities and localities, this new economic policy takes shape in large-scale infrastructure projects, the skilling and flexibilization of labour (local labour-market policies), and the loosening up of spatial and commercial regulations to make them more feasible for new private investments. In this way, through this New Urban Policy (NUP), cities keep up with the globalization movement and manage to occupy their own prosperous niche in the new urban hierarchy of production and labour.

In Chapters 1 and 2 we criticized the New Economic Policy (NEP) and its local credo (NUP), i.e. the New Urban Policy. We argued that a poor understanding of its nature inspires the pursuit of an economic development policy as a free rider on the waves of globalization. First of all, the real impact of globalization is misunderstood in many respects. Only in the domain of international finance and political governance, are we entitled to talk of a new phenomenon. As far as 'global competition' is concerned, indeed, the world economy seems to have returned to economic neo-colonialism: social protection and international solidarity with developing countries are increasingly sacrificed to the desiderata of international market 'wild life'. Naturally, this economic neo-colonialism is only a socio-political and not a technico-organizational retro movement, as it adopts contemporary forms enabled by recent progress in financial and management technology and computing and communication (Chapter 2).

Moreover, even if relevant as an explanation for intensified international competition, the role of globalization in the crisis of local economies should not be overstated. For most localities in the Western world, the seeds of crisis and destruction were already present in the Fordist mode of regulation. By adopting the NEP remedy, the crisis has often intensified. This is visibly the case where local authorities withdrew from public spending in traditional socio-economic projects (social services, public housing, public education, etc.), and decided to play all their cards in NUP. We argued that 'going NUP' represents a major threat to the future of urban society. For in many cities this harsh form of neo-liberal local economic policy can be identified as a principal cause of the accelerated decline of fragile neighbourhoods, the negative catalyst of polarization in urban labour-markets, the destroyer of traditional modes of integration, socialization, and economic organization in cities and their neighbourhoods (compare with Van Berkel 1997).

Therefore, as an alternative to New Economic Policy in the city, in Chapters 4 and 5 we made a strong case in favour of Integrated Area Development (IAD), which is not only expected to glue together the pieces of the socio-economy of the Fordist epoch, but also to change the view of local development strategies. Instead of stressing the role of market forces to create human prosperity for all layers of the population, IAD focuses on social innovation as a driving force for renewed local development. Social innovation in at least two senses: satisfaction of basic needs, especially of the most deprived populations and neighbourhoods; and innovation in human interaction forming new social relations which enable the co-ordination of action and co-operation in innovative local development projects. Both dimensions culminate in a renewed sense of responsibility which bypasses the traditional meaning of 'public administration' and the new but somewhat paternalistic 'social citizenship' policy by local 'government' in favour of a dynamic view of responsibility, much more in accordance with the multidimensional local 'governance'. The latter involves shared tasks of the discovery of needs—those of the most deprived in the first place, contributing to the revival and the improvement of grass-roots democracy (for example, encouraging communication between all sectors of civil society), the transformation of public decision-making systems, the inclusion of cultural and social values in the administration of the *polis*, etc. In this way, in Chapters 4 and 5, we distance ourselves from an administrative view of local governance. 'New' governance is defined as new modes of admin-istration, dealing with new political agendas and involving 'new' partners in accordance with a new style of social interaction (horizontal communication, grass-roots democracy, empowerment of local communities).

Our belief in the IAD approach, based on this new view of governance in which social innovation stands central, is pragmatic. It is based on the case studies which we have presented in this book and on our critical reading of the literature on alternative development which we cite (Douthwaite, Ekins, Friedmann, Perna, etc.). This evidence shows that alternative local develop-ment strategies based on social innovation are often effective.

6.1. The need for global governance

But 'new' local governance alone lives a hard life. All authors preoccupied by the challenge of local governance are more or less concerned about the wider environment or global structure in which this 'local renaissance' can take place. If they recognize that many local authorities, by adopting NUP, share responsibility for growing polarization in many cities, they are even more aware that the evolution of the regional, national, and international institu-tions, in which the local must evolve and act, has certainly fostered local devel-opment patterns.

A brief reminder of 'macro' evolutions which led to local destitution offers a good starting-point for the discussion on desired institutional changes which together could provide the foot-prints leading towards a new global govern-ance.

6.1.1. Beggar your neighbour or leave it to the uncles?

The *adagi* of the New Economic Policy are well known. And still it would be an untruthful representation of the policy context if we portrayed economic reg-ulation in the globalizing economy as based on the complete withdrawal of national states in favour of a few international watchdogs monitoring the cor-rect implementation of a market environment in which decentralized eco-nomic agents (firms, local public and private authorities) accomplish their job by pursuing individual or negotiated self-interest. Inspired by Dryzek (1999) when he talks about international political systems and discourse, we could argue that international economic regulation these days rests on two pillars: Hobbesian anarchy, where individual states seek to maximize their share using the old Fordist remedies of national political power and economic expansion-ism; and market liberalism, where the action is left to economic actors such as corporations, bankers, and consumers, and where supranational economic institutions (IMF, World Bank, WTO) have the limited functions of preserving free market mechanisms and guaranteeing sound financial markets.

In the reality of international economic relations, both pictures are intimately intertwined. If, for the legitimization of the free world market, 'market liberalism' passes better as a 'global discourse' than 'economic anarchy', a general appraisal of international economic regulation shows that 'practice' is genuinely less 'global' and more 'national' than the 'global discourse' advertises. In this way, the liberalization policies which many great nations pursue show more similarities with the 'beggar your neighbour' policies of the 1920s than we would expect. In the 1920s there was the conviction that the maintenance of the gold standard and the protection of the currency provided the basis 'to equalize conditions of competition amongst the nations so that trade might be liberated without danger to standards of living' (Polanyi 1944: 26), and

Although everybody agreed that stable currencies ultimately depended upon the freeing of trade, all except dogmatic free traders knew that measures had to be taken immediately which would inevitably restrict foreign trade and foreign payments. (Polanyi 1944: 27)

This led to a spiral of policies of protectionism, quota, import moratoria, restrictive measures of all kind, with the sole purpose of increasing market share at the expense of one's neighbour. The obsession with the gold standard, meant to liberalize trade, thus led to one of the most typical periods of 'national anarchy' in international trade, which eventually led to one of the biggest depressions in the history of capitalism, and meant the end of the gold standard and the collapse or reform of the international institutions (Haute finance, League of Nations) and national institutions (the 'nineteenth-century' liberal states) that went with it (Polanyi 1944).

It may seem odd to draw parallels between the 1920s and the national economic policy and free market liberalism of the so-called post-Fordist period, said to have begun in the mid-1970s. Still, similarities are striking. First of all, there has been an accelerated movement towards trade liberalization through the different GATT rounds and the politico-economic disciplining of economic nations that sought relief in protectionism and autarchy (including the socialist countries). This movement was first decelerated, then speeded up by the collapse in 1973 of the Bretton Woods agreement and the Fixed Exchange Rate system, which had regulated international monetary and financial transactions under the Fordist regime. In the years following, Western states lost their grip on the traditional means to control inflation (price control, income policy: the so-called micro-economic policies) and relied increasingly on monetary instruments to check price levels. Although the international monetary regime was quite unbalanced, with floating dollar, yen, and pound sterling, starting towards the end of the 1970s, within the European Union and led by Germany and the Netherlands, an increasing number of nations began to follow a hard currency policy, supported by high interest rates, intervention in the wage formation, and disciplined public spending. This policy created huge unemployment, but was justified by the 'external constraint': the necessity to check the national in comparison with the international price level and to avoid structural imbalances in net inflow of capital and factor income (compare with Notermans 1997).

Today, social and environmental deregulation has become part of the competitive challenge. With prices in the Western economy almost stable, and the pressure from the New Industrial Nations rising, flexibilization of the labour force and the loosening up of national environmental regulations have become part of the national economic policy (for the USA, see Faber 1998). At the same time the active relocation of heavily polluting industries to less developed nations can without doubt be interpreted as part of a strategy to improve the national competitive position in the framework of anarchic world capitalism.

In the same vein, if the 'national anarchy' of the most powerful economic nations is reproduced already in the post-war international monetary organizations (IMF, World Bank as dominated by the USA), this is even more the case in recently created international organizations monitoring compliance with the standards of free world trade (WTO) and good state behaviour (OECD, G7). It is obvious that these organizations are either exclusive clubs of the most powerful nations and their strategic allies (e.g. G7), or that these nations dominate these organizations (e.g. the IMF and the World Bank disciplining weaker or smaller nations according to the US view of the minimalist state).

Neither is the often defended picture that, with the establishment of the 'free trade order' at the world level, the main industries—the remaining 'national champions'—of the biggest economic nations would lose their national affinity correct. These corporations remain in global economic power or see their national power 'globalized' thanks to the explicit or implicit support of 'their' strong nation states (Dicken 1994).

Interpreting three institutional realities at the world level—national anarchy, uneven power among nation states with a tentative collusion among the strongest, and increasing free trade in the world market—and one dominant discourse, namely that of 'market liberalism', helps to explain a rather complicated picture of international economic regulation and national social and economic policy:

• Contemporary international finance and capital flows can only partly be compared with a 'jungle' because the law of the strongest is predominant. It is a fairly regulated jungle in which major banks and corporations, supranational organizations, and leading nations have a definite stake, i.e. to pursue security and reduce risk in the money and capital markets, and to enhance freedom of trade flows, especially in the markets in which leading economic nations are dominating: high technology-based products, producer services, intangibles of all kinds, etc.

- 'Some [national] markets are more liberated than others' (Capital farm 1998): nations with a weak economic basis, with less developed regulations in the domain of labour rights and environmental protection, or which are less 'administratively equipped' to implement laws and regulations, easily become economically colonized as branch plant economies and as markets of leading economic nations and their corporations. Typical cases here are Mexico for the USA, Eastern and Central Europe for Germany, the USA, and other leading economic nations, South-east Asia for Japan.

- Within the changing regulation of the international economy, nation states cede power to international organizations. But there is again significant asymmetry in the power that is ceded, and the disciplining of nations as exerted by international organizations (Altvater 1997; Cuyvers and Rayp 1997). That the institutionalization of market liberalism would lead to a global disciplining of national economies has proven to be a fantasy. Developing countries which are strongly indebted must live up to the bible of the IMF and the World Bank, even if the application of the imposed restrictions pushes two digit percentages of the domestic population into extreme poverty, as is the case of Indonesia today. But other countries such as Belgium and Italy, with a strong economic basis, a high standard of living, and a long-standing capitalist tradition of high productivity, may get away with gradual reduction of the public debt, while hardly lowering the average standard of living of the population.

- The national implementation of international disciplining rules and budgetary orthodoxy varies strongly and cannot exclusively be explained in economic terms. Why is it that a rich country like the USA has a much weaker social protection shield for its population than a somewhat less rich country like France? Why do in some countries social policy goals receive a higher priority, while the public budget space is as large or even smaller than in others? Endogenous socio-political strength and institutional trajectories of the nations in question play an important role here. The differences in approach cannot be explained in terms of position in the world market. There is in other words even in this era of globalization sufficient national autonomy to tackle similar challenges in different ways. This obviously means that various philosophies and practices with respect to local development are possible. We will come back to this issue in section 6.3.

6.1.2. An alternative view of the global

Contemporary society is not only living the euphoria—the NEP future—or the negative consequences—increasing social, economic, and political polarization; the economic colonization of culture and the human mind; the destruction of nature—of free market arrogance. Simultaneously with it, in reaction to it, or in the stream of autonomous civilian initiatives, different approaches and practices, be they 'alternative', 'supplementary', 'turning down', or 'ignoring' market institutions, are tried out. Since the end of the 1970s, an increasing number of authors have called for some more or less explicit forms of international co-ordination, regulation, or governance to drive agendas of change.

Satisfaction of basic needs in 'all worlds'

Already conscious of the problem that international capitalist trade and investments were destroying a large part of the local production potential in developing countries, several reports (Palme report 1982; Brandt reports 1980, 1983) made a plea in favour of economic development in developing countries, so that they would rediscover the possibilities to provide better for their own needs. In particular, an appeal was made for financial transfers from the rich to the poor countries. But this approach failed because in these reports, especially in the Brandt report, there was no scrutiny of the quality of the desired production and governance models, or a honest analysis of the basic mechanisms of unequal development in the world (Ekins 1992: 29). The Palme report was primarily focused on world peace and security problems, including that of economic security. Significant progress was made in the Brundtland report of 1987, taking up many of the themes in the Brandt reports and recognizing the importance of fairer trade and the creation of social organizations that would carry the development endeavours. The Brundtland report advocated a sustainable development process, in which the local populations play an important role. The report was written in a climate of long-lasting economic crisis in the industrialized countries. Similarities between uneven development in the First and the Third World were discovered and the search for more solid grass-roots development models and the *international conditions* that could favour their proliferation received a new impetus. It is in this climate that an older pioneering report by the Dag Hammarskjöld Foundation (1975) entitled *What Now? Another Development*, which we cited in Chapter 4, maintains its full relevance.

Fair trade

One of these conditions is 'fair trade', i.e. trade in which the distribution of income received from the production and trade of exchanged goods and services grants an at least fair income to all workers involved in the chain that goes from the production of the raw materials to the selling of the product to the final consumer or investor. In his brilliant little book on *Fair Trade*, Tonino Perna (1998) explains the roots of ethical production and fair trade.[1] To make

---

[1] Fair trade shops or so-called 'World Shops' were launched in the Netherlands. The first shop was opened in 1969 in Brekelen, in the south of the Netherlands. Today, there are 3,500 world shops in 15 European countries. Statistically, their importance is not so clear. But they carry the call for fair trade between the North and the South: opportunities for all people in the world to receive a fair share in the final sale price of the products they produce.

fair trade possible, consciousness-raising and political information and education on the injustice of unequal exchange and the possibilities of alternative
trade organizations and production systems are necessary. In the vein of the
socio-political openness of the late 1960s and the 1970s, the fair trade movement (such as SOS World Trade created in the Netherlands in 1959) became
part of one stream together with the ecological movement and the movements
for human rights and emancipation. In this way, fair trade was connected to
ecological production and models of more equitable human organization in
production (see also the Brundtland report and the Hammerskjold
Foundation report cited above). But there are dangers with the fair trade logic
as it is propagated and applied today. One is that it remains too focused on
elaborating alternatives to the unequal exchange imposed by the North on the
South, with the danger of neglecting the basic unequal exchange between the
capitalist and the working class throughout the capitalist world, the North
included. Another danger is that parallel trade systems are developed which
leave the structural injustice inherent in the capitalist trade system unharmed.[2]

Ecological balance

Another condition to make alternative needs satisfaction models work is that
production and trade become more ecological. The disruptive effects of large-
scale capitalist and state socialist production and trade systems on the environment have been widely described. The international and national
geography of unequal environmental damage is becoming increasingly
known. At the international level, 'national' ecological disasters spill over into
international ecological problems: the devastation of the rain forest, the
exportation of toxic waste and of heavily polluting production activities to
developing countries, and the spread of nuclear radiation (Chernobyl) are well
known. The environment also becomes 'globally poisoned' as we know from
the generalized automobile traffic problem, the destruction of the ozone layer,
the exhaustion of fossil energy, etc. Moreover, international deregulation of
trade and capital flows will speed up the process of global environmental
decaying (Low and Gleeson 1999: 184–5). But also within countries there is a
strong geographical correlation between the living areas of poorer income
groups and the zones in which polluting activities are concentrated (production, heavy traffic, waste disposal, . . .).

  Since the 1980s ecological movements have risen at all spatial levels: from
the global Greenpeace and WWF to the national environmental associations
and the local environmental protection committees. The agendas of these
organizations may vary according to their 'spatial connection' and there are
also significant differences in their social orientation; but all of them are of
significant relevance in the struggle for the quality of human life. Moreover,

---

[2] The latter observation is particularly relevant in a world where 'fair trade' represents only
0.008% of total world trade (figures from Perna 1998: 105).

these organizations have developed new forms of international networking, which can be considered as innovative for their own purpose, i.e. to organize with the objective of improving environmental protection, but which can also serve as examples for other groups or networks which are searching for modes of organization and operation.

Democracy

One of the other main problems of our time, in addition to unfair trade and the destruction of the ecological environment, is the poor state of democracy. There can be no improvement in the basic existential condition of excluded populations if they are not involved in democratic decision-making systems. But how can they be involved if democracy as a system is increasingly failing because of the hollowing out of the political role of the state by the globalizing market forces (Altvater 1997), and the loss-of-grip of the national state on the ecological space (which becomes increasingly international—a challenge for global governance)? The national democratic state is increasingly becoming an economic broker for international capital and a negotiating agent in the establishment of new international regulations in various spheres (international trade, money and capital markets, biosphere, etc.). Its power to protect the economic and social rights of its citizens is slowly crumbling away. Although this phenomenon should not be exaggerated, national social security systems are more or less exposed to the logic of international competition and its pressure towards social dumping (Cuyvers and Rayp 1997). The entrepreneurial role of the state is invented by, or inherited from, the national state by the regional and local state authorities, whose democratic structures are still in the making (Moulaert, Swyngedouw, and Wilson 1988).

Within this institutional reshifting of power among different levels of state authority, special systems of participation are needed to include deprived groups of the population in the democratic process. An open debate on the future of democracy is underway.

Power

This is probably the key variable in the whole political exercise on governance at different spatial levels. What is the sense of working to improve the natural and social environment, to create systems of fair trade, to innovate in democratic decision-making if capitalist accumulation continues to roll on as it has for the last two centuries? And what is the point of brandishing grass-roots democracy if the reality is that the authoritarian national central state has been replaced by an asymmetrical model of world governance dominated by the USA, Japan, and Germany? These questions are the destroyers of political innovation, for it does indeed need a strong and global political power to countervail world capitalism and the new political entente of the G7. Investing in these countervailing forces is a very delicate matter today, and for several reasons. First, the new social movements are too focused on their own targets: an improvement in the ecosystem, fair trade outside the capitalist realm, development and grass-roots democracy at the local level. Second, the post-modern criticism of modernity and its acquisitions such as labour unions, mixed economy capitalism, the social welfare state with social security, health services, and education for the entire population, lacks nuance. Fordist or post-Keynesian strategies to contain capitalist development and the democratizing of the capitalist state will continue to play an important role in socio-political change. To deny this, is a post-modern misinterpretation of history, which will hopefully be corrected in the near future (Moulaert, Sekia, and Boyabe 1999).

6.2. Investing in social capital

The discussion about new international governance involves basically two categories of problems. The first includes the organization of governance, the second its agenda. Let us begin with the second.

Today, there is a strong need for accurate symbols to portray the message for a new global governance. One way is to return to the original meaning of 'capital' as structures 'of prime importance'. The best known form of capital is 'private capital', which in modern Greek is translated as 'idiotic' capital, self-centred capital, operating at the expense of other forms of capital which are more important to the future of humanity, but which are not recognized as such.

Following an argument by O'Hara (1998) who extrapolates T. Veblen's analysis of collective wealth (Veblen 1899), we could broaden the discussion on local innovation by referring to different types of capital and the relations between them. As O'Hara states: 'Capital or wealth, generally speaking, is the dynamic stock of durable structures, whatever those structures may be' (1998: 174a.f.). He distinguishes between four types of capital:

- Ecological capital: 'the stock of all environmental and ecological resources. It is a dynamic stock involving the biosphere, the gene pool, plant and animal species; the weather, the cycles of nature, and the physical environment' (1998: 174).

- Social (or institutional) capital 'comprises those norms, mores, relationships and organizational arrangements which help to bond people together. Some minimal degree of trust, respect, dignity and communication between people are necessary with this form of capital' (1998: 177).

- Human capital 'is usually related to those skills and knowledge that are capable of general application, although "firm specific" human capital and "learning by doing" are of considerable importance' (1998: 181).

- Private business capital: this category includes 'the creation of durable structures within corporations, such as machinery, factories, tools, warehouses, buildings, and inventories' (1998: 184).

O'Hara's classification is not quite coherent, because parts of ecological, social, and human capital have been privatized and belong to private business capital. Still, the subdivision suggests a number of interesting discussions about the synergies, destruction, and substitutions that are possible between the various types of capital. It is well known that business capital has destroyed a large part of ecological and organizational capital. Moreover, trade-offs between various types of capital are not just a matter of preferences, but touch the core of the organization of the economy and society. Regions and cities with a qualitatively outstanding social capital, or/and a good ecological system can have a higher level of well-being than other regions with much vaster business capital stock and a higher level of income (the examples cited by O'Hara). There is a first lesson to be drawn here on the governance of regions and localities: local development strategies carrying basic needs will only work in regions with a governance rooted in the socio-cultural heritage of the localities that seeks to develop new modes of democratic participation and social solidarity. Such a local governance structure will enable the development potential. But it will also be the basis on which to countervail the course of capitalist development and to force autocratic state structures on to new democratic avenues.

6.3. Organizing for change

Returning now to the levels of governance, in particular to the interaction between local and global governance, it is clear that the existing mechanisms of global political and economic governance are not exactly the pampering cradle of Integrated Area Development. Even a dynamic, creative, and democratic local governance structure will not be a sufficient institutional carrier of alternative development at the local level. The following changes in governance dynamics must be fostered.

6.3.1. Promotion of new governance styles

The proliferation of movements in the fields of human rights, social economy, ecology, fair trade, etc., has provided us with experiences and evaluations of new styles of governance. From the micro-scale of society, the neighbourhood, or the small rural community, to the global geography of ecological and fair trade organizations, new forms of communication, collaboration, and administration applying to various agendas of human emancipation have been developed. In Chapters 4 and 5, but particularly in the latter, we have illustrated this for the social economy and alternative development of neighbourhoods. Similar organizational and institutional capital is available from fair trade networks and shops, from grass-roots and global environmental movements, from civil rights organizations, etc. The knowledge and experience is available and it is increasingly shared in networks bringing together communities and organizations from different countries and regions. Basically, what is going on is experimentation with democracy. As Dryzek writes:

Democracy is an open-ended project, such that a key feature of democratic society is experimentation with what democracy can mean. (1999)

6.3.2. Linking scales of governance

But it is an open-ended agenda that is today confronted with the hollowing out of the Fordist model, and with the challenge of global governance, and, even more so, the elaboration of efficient links between levels of governance. The ongoing debate and institutional changes in the realm of ecological movements and the search for ecological justice and environmental democracy is quite instructive from this point of view. Low and Gleeson (1999) report on the proposal:

to create a 'directly elected World Environmental Council and an International Court of the Environment'. Both have already been foreshadowed. A Global Environmental Organisation created under the UN with comparable authority to the World Trade Organization has been proposed. (1999: 191)

The direct election of representatives of 'peoples and communities' (1999: 190 a.f.) and of environmental NGOs as new political subjects (Altvater 1997: 22) are a worthwhile alternative to state representation and may offer a key leverage for solving the problem of the linking of scales in the new governance dynamics. International networks of NGOs are also active in the fields of fair trade, gender emancipation, human rights, social economy, etc. In this way important innovative segments of civil society have become actors in the movement for the renewal of global governance.

6.3.3. Dealing with power

But Altvater pours salt in the wound when he writes that:

Therefore the assumption that an international civil society could emerge without heavy social and political conflicts that would alter the relations between market actors, governments of nation states, NGO's, international organizations etc., is naive. Global governance is not an institutional setting for the global regulation of global problems (such as drug traffic, debts, AIDS, migration etc.) but an arena of conflicts waged by social, economic and political actors. The outcome is uncertain and not predictable, since it is the result of a chaotic social, political and economic process. (Altvater 1997: 23)

The new global governance, with all its interlinked spatial scales, will be based on the forces of production and creation available in contemporary society. An organic perspective cannot be avoided here. For it does not make sense to transplant new models of democracy and civil control on to the debris of the Fordist society, as a strategy to solve the problems of this society. There are several reasons for this.

First of all, the Fordist society is still very much alive and quite dynamic in its own reproduction. Any unbiased observer of the transformation of Fordism will confirm the strengthening of monopoly capital—that it is increasingly organized in small units or small firms does not make the difference to the capitalist social relations of production (Martinelli and Schoenberger 1992)—and the reinforcement of control structures in the political and economic domain. The latter becomes increasingly clear from the role which business firms play as powerful citizens in the post-Fordist political system. Business logic feeds the heart of political regulation, as we illustrated in Chapters 1 and 2, and earlier in this chapter. Post-Fordism is built from the solid materials of Fordism, which are spatially flexible and controlled by financially concentrated private capital and solid market-friendly political authorities at various spatial scales (regions, nations, continents, or world). No new governance can be created without entering into confrontation with this 'post'-Fordist reality, or without mobilizing social forces produced by Fordism (Moulaert, Sekia, and Boyabe 1999).

Second, democracy has been transformed by Fordism. The political constituency of Fordist society consists of citizens with a decent income (as provided by the Fordist wage–labour relationship) and who are more or less well connected to the socio-political institutions leading the regulation of society: unions, political parties, socio-cultural organizations. The crisis of Fordism pushed large portions of this typical political clientele into unemployment or precarious job situations. The bonds of trust between increasingly large numbers of the population and the institutions of democracy were disrupted, in the first place because Fordism was no longer capable of providing them with acceptable material well-being. Increasingly too the 'Fordist polity' is challenged for its incapacity to deal with environmental problems and unequal exchange at the world level. Therefore, new forms of democracy should take over the Fordist agenda of redistribution of wealth and address the problems of inequality and environmental destruction caused by Fordism.

An important aspect of the transformation of the Fordist political system is the loss of power of the national state in economic policy. Micro-economic policy of redistribution and decentralized price control has been sacrificed to macro-economic strong currency and anti-inflation policy, as we have seen earlier in this chapter. The instruments for this policy are high real interest rates and (or) public budget discipline, two factors which constrain the possibilities of local authorities to lead their own decentralized development and social services policies. With the creation of the EMU and the unique currency euro in the European Union, this will become even more tangible. Interest rate policy and public deficit control are now delegated to a higher level of governance, and can no longer be used by national states as instruments of expansionary policy and job creation. The only remaining instruments to this purpose are therefore investment policy (the entrepreneurial state) and the activation of micro-economic distribution policy. But the latter means that the real redistribution of income that under Fordism could always be so carefully avoided by high growth and creeping inflation, will become *incontournable* in the new macro-economic regime.

Third, *can the devil also be the angel?* Can UN international organizations such as the IMF and the World Bank, which at present squeeze poor countries and are responsible for the death of tens of thousands in these countries, also patronize global governance fostering ecological justice, respect for human rights, equal exchange among national and regional economies? Our opinion here is 'no', unless their policy priorities are structurally challenged. *In concreto* this could mean that the World Bank should only support investment programmes which are built on the principles of grass-roots governance, equal exchange, ecological balance, and respect for human rights—in the social and ecological sense of the term and not in the US euphemistic meaning, where the freedom of speech is literally linked to the freedom to become capitalist slave labour or even the freedom to starve. It could also mean that the IMF should adapt its monetary disciplining tools to the income situation in the countries concerned.

The fear of modernist or Fordist authoritarian structures is all too visible in the formulation of proposals for the new forms of governance. There is a strong aversion to a world state that would have the authority to impose a halt to excesses of environmental and social destruction; there is a hesitation to go beyond the level of negotiation and effective control and to provide the new governance agents with power to penalize; but at the same time there is an awareness that without power exertion nothing will change (Low and Gleeson 1999). Therefore, political pragmatism in the development of new modes of governance is necessary. The creation of new organizations and networks should happen by mobilizing the forces of change which Fordism created: unions, political parties, social movements, etc., are themselves embodiments of the struggle between conservative and progressive forces about the future of socio-economic and socio-political life. This is not the place to provide an exhaustive account of the osmosis between Fordist organizations and so-called post-modern change movements. First of all, many of these movements are faithful children of Fordist institutions issuing from the change movements of the 1960s and 1970s (Moulaert, Sekia, and Boyabe 1999). And second—if not a corollary of the previous point—there is a significant overlap between the progressive personnel of unions, political organizations, and the change movements in the various domains already noted. These developments are on the one hand organic: a society should produce its own change factors. On the other hand they reflect strategic pragmatism: without coalitions with the change forces of the Fordist era, no countervailing forces capable of changing the development agendas and the governance dynamics are possible.

6.3.4. New development agenda and discourse

When working on new development agendas, it is therefore not sufficient to focus on the 'personal' or 'localist' scale, to foster new movements and projects, and to cling to an undialectical critique of modernity. If there can be a consensus on building up alternatives from below, there should emerge a shared understanding that the following ingredients are necessary:

(*a*) *bottom-up strategies.* These are not necessarily local. This has been clearly demonstrated by the environmental movement, whose most successful actions were performed at several places at the same time or by multinational teams in a strategic space (e.g. in the Pacific, against the French nuclear tests);

(*b*) local strategies should look for *communication and association* with agents and organizations in the local communities, even if this means 'involvement' with the structures of Fordism. In fact, some of the most successful local development actions presented in the previous chapters were led in collaboration with local and regional authorities, unions, progressive personalities and groups in political parties;

(*c*) local change movements should collaborate to establish *regional, national, and international organizations and networks, with different functionalities*: communication between different initiatives (exchange of information on experiences), organization and co-ordination of joint programmes, confrontation with power structures at different spatial levels. This is why the agendas of networks of NGOs in any of the cited change domains involve simultaneously the development of a global discourse of change, political organization and confrontation, organization, and proliferation of change models;

(*d*) *coalitions with unions, political parties*, etc., are of prime importance in leading the struggle for change of existing global, national, and regional institutions. As already suggested, the roles of the IMF, the World Bank, and the WTO must drastically change. These organizations should create stability in world monetary, financial, and trade relations, set up mechanisms for redistribution among countries and collaborate to create or improve world governance organizations in the domain of ecology, equal development opportunities, human rights, etc. It is within these organizations that capitalism should change its religion from quantitative growth to qualitative development.

But these types of change coalitions must also continue to play a role on national territories. We argued in the first chapters that despite globalization national and local authorities maintain a sufficient degree of freedom to choose among development objectives. Redistribution policy remains possible, maybe more so in a European Monetary Union than ever before.

Priorities in ecological spatial planning, in democratic cultural policy, in social education, etc., can be determined within a national context. But these priorities must be defended by change coalitions, and not solely by 'frontier organizations', which may have the ideas and the know-how to come to the fore with alternative agendas, but lack the power to implement them.

6.4. Integrated Area Development and governance

This book dealt in the first place with the analysis of development trajectories in depressed localities and with the Integrated Area Development (IAD) model as an alternative strategy for local renaissance. The strength of Integrated Area Development lies in its focus on social innovation: the basic needs of the population come first and bottom-up socio-organizational innovation is essential to meet them. The discussion on socio-organizational innovation was mainly around the notion of local governance: organization, communication, and decision-making procedures within the projects and the communities, and with the other development agents at the local, regional, national, and EU level.

The reflections in this chapter warn us that a successful prolongation and proliferation of IAD experiences will not be sufficient to solve the restructuring crisis of localities. There is also a need for renewal of 'global governance', while the links between various scales of governance need to be rethought and reconstructed. And it is of utmost importance that new development targets be linked to changes in governance dynamics. Or, in the terminology of IAD: both types of social innovation must be combined to make IAD effective. To close this book, a number of guidelines for the future implementation of IAD are left to the reader for further reflection.

First, the development agenda of the IAD should be multidimensional. Ecological, socio-cultural, organizational aspects of production systems, and democratic modes of interaction between change agents should all be part of the agenda. Otherwise the change content of the project can become very ambiguous.

Second, if local governance structures seem quite well developed in most of the projects we studied, there is a lack of continuous communication between similar projects and experiences. Of course, the EU Poverty programmes and the URBAN programme have facilitated such communication structures; but there remains a lack of permanence in these programmes, and therefore a need for the IAD organizations to improve their own global networks of information and globalization.

Third, the political interaction with the 'Fordist forces of change' remains too casual, or too project focused. What is needed is the establishment of a political agenda to support IAD at a regional, national, and European level. This involves, as we have already seen, changes in priorities of public spending and redistribution policy, enabling the funding of investments and seed money for co-operative enterprises meeting ecological, social, and political criteria. But it also requires changes in the legal frameworks regulating the creation of corporations and associations, as well as their support organizations.

Fourth, we miss a 'global discourse' on the social economy: the meaningfulness of IAD should be explained as a key element in the transformation of the capitalist economy into a co-operative economy. For this purpose, links with the anarchist and utopian literature on co-operative production models (Perna 1998; Achterhuis 1998), but also with the long history of co-operative enterprises, should be established. These ideas and experiences should be confronted with the contemporary change ventures of the ecological, fair trade, and human rights movements. Such a global discourse should be carried on by a large movement in civil society uniting all groups concerned with the deterioration of the quality of economic, social, and political life.

Fifth, the management of co-operative enterprises and governance systems should become a core topic in the study curricula of economics and business administration schools. The existing courses on the management of not-for-profit organizations do not match this need. They should be complemented by topics on alternative development, levels and types of governance, grass-roots democracy practice, and the place of the economic in social development. Education is the basic institution where mentalities and attitudes towards social development can be changed. And although formal education cannot replace the educational impact of the household or life community, its re-orientation towards the training of concerned world citizens and managers will be of great help.

APPENDIX
METHODOLOGY FOR THE STUDY OF
LOCAL DEVELOPMENT

The first part concerns quantitative data. These can normally be obtained from Censuses (Population, Enterprises, etc.). Census data are commonly available at the level of 'statistical geographical units' (every city or urban area consists of several 'statistical geographical units'). Other data can usually be acquired from National Employment (or Unemployment) Offices, Chambers of Commerce or other institutions centralizing professional enquiries.

The second part consists of qualitative information.

Both types of information are used to construct a 'locality file'.

1. Quantitative Data

For the quantitative data, we collected information at the smallest spatial level possible, and the next higher spatial level (City, Agglomeration, Region, etc.) taking the local community (quarter, neighbourhood) under investigation as a lower bound. We tried to reproduce them for the last three censuses and included the useful data in the locality file under the appropriate heading.

The following headings for quantitative data are recommended:

1.1. Demography, migration, mobility, usual pathologies

1.2. Housing and land fragmentation

1.3. Sectoral structure of employment, VA, output, investments, *with detail for the x leading sectors (indicate level of sectoral disaggregation)*

1.4. Labour-market: employment, unemployment, commuting, and migration

1.5. Educational system

1.6. Main activities: economic and employment data

1.7. Financial and investment flows

For each heading and variable, a clear reference to the closest geographical unit as well as a definition of the variable should be provided.

2. Qualitative Data

2.1. Brief socio-economic and socio-cultural history of the community

This section should provide a general historical picture of the locality. It is meant as an introduction to the following sections.

2.2. Political and administrative system at different spatial levels

This section should summarize how the public sector is organized and how the different spatial levels of that sector affect the political and administrative structure, behaviour, and action at the local level. It is, of course, very important to understand: (a) the possibilities

for local development initiatives at the local level; (b) how the existing political and administrative institutions (could) foster collaborations or (could) hamper local economic development initiatives.

It is very difficult to put these elements into a strictly formatted structure. A loose format looks evident. But essential information must be presented and can be collected under the headings mentioned further on. Summary articles exist for many countries. They may serve as a basis to fill part of the headings.

Note that the understanding of how existing institutional structures, administrative behaviour, public actions, etc., affect the efficacy of local action is very important as a basis for the study of local development potentials.

Each heading should contain the main historical developments, from a relevant time perspective.

2.2.1. Main laws and regulations in the institutional framework for local economic development initiatives by the public and private sector, or in private–public co-operation.

2.2.2. Division of competencies among different political and administrative levels with respect to domains which affect local economic development. Such domains are:

> labour-market;
> education and training;
> technology;
> investments;
> R. & D.;
> housing;
> infrastructure;
> tourism.

It is useful to provide columns to indicate political and administrative agents as they intervene in these domains, and to show which instruments they use.

2.2.3. Public authorities intervening in local economic development.

This entry is meant to elaborate on the authorities which are of greatest importance for local economic development initiatives.

2.2.4. Division of competencies in local economic development initiatives among authorities at different spatial scales: who controls whom and to which effect? (blocking power, benevolent support, collaborations, networks, etc.).

2.2.5. Networking—collaboration with the European Union.

2.3. Short description of local authorities

This should include the organization, competencies with respect to economic development (relative autonomy?), collaboration with authorities at a higher-order spatial level, and the quality of the local political delivery system.

Here, we are talking in terms of political authorities at the local or just-above-the local level intervening in different areas related to local economic development: municipalities or groupings of municipalities, possibly district authorities, etc.

Again, relevant historical events must be included in the analysis in this section.

2.3.1. Municipalities, etc. A short description of how they are functionally organized and what their competencies are with respect to local economic development (*possible overlap with section 2.2.2*). Which divisions, services, neighbourhood municipalities, etc., are the most involved in local economic development organization and action?

2.3.2. Collaboration among authorities in different localities and at higher spatial levels: the role of local authorities in networking for (local) economic development:

> who takes the initiatives?
> public/private collaboration?
> local/regional/national/supranational collaboration?
> in which domains (list in section 2.2)?

2.3.3. Quality of local policy delivery systems:

> democratic content of decision-making;
> professional preparation of decision-making;
> available instruments: financial, management, interest groups;
> affiliations of functionaries and local politicians.

2.3.4. Local authorities and social dynamics:

> relationships between socio-economic organizations and local authorities;
> social, political, and socio-cultural movements in interaction with local authorities:
>
> > mobilization and conflicts on issues;
> >
> > democratic content of local politics: links between political representatives, high level functionaries, organizations, and movements;
>
> impact of movements on efficacy of policy delivery, outside traditional political and administrative channels: mobilization for support and counter-action, spontaneous agency for support and local action and of policy measures, administrative behaviour, and actions.

2.4. Socio-economic regulation at different spatial levels

This should include professional organizations, Labour Unions, Chambers of Commerce, state administrations, private organizations of diverse types, and address the following issues:

Balance/imbalance between formal and informal regulation: how important is the question for the locality under investigation?

Formal economic regulation: is this completely obedient to existing state and socio-professional regulation?

Informal economic regulation at relevant spatial levels:
> market organization for final and intermediary products;
> labour relations;
> land and housing allocation.

2.5. Leading economic activities

This should describe economic and financial information; enterprise files for leading enterprises; reference to regulatory mechanisms proper to the sector; business culture; the role of different local and supra-local assets; spatial embeddedment.

The definition of a 'leading activity' used in this context is somewhat unorthodox, because it distances itself from the traditional approach which defines leading activities in accordance with the contemporary regime of accumulation (Boyer 1986c). A territorial approach to the articulation among regimes of accumulation and forms of development leads to an a priori different notion of a leading sector, i.e. the sector that drives the local economy. This sector can be a sector stemming from a previous regime of accumulation or some older form of it; or it can belong to the informal sector, etc. In most localities, there is a number of leading activities. In our sample, many of these activities are in decline. Informality can play a very important role in leading activities.

2.5.1. Brief histories of leading economic activities in the locality in the post-war period

This should be a mixed qualitative–quantitative history of leading economic sectors. Information concerns the three principal sectors (at least this number in case the sectoral structure is rather dispersed) of the localities: a short description of the nature of the activities—trends in employment, investment, production, and innovation—the importance of the local labour-market (some information on migration and commuting)—information on the main firms—information on the capital structure of the main enterprises (also on its geographical dimensions)—the causes of decline and prosperity.

In the event that informal economic activities play a major role or that informality is significant in 'formal sectors', additional information should be provided on the organization of the work process: the putting out system, domestic labour, illegal workshops, avoidance of labour laws, etc., as well as relationships between different forms of organization.

2.5.2. Contemporary leading economic activities: quantitative economic indicators

Preferably, there should be coherence between the quantitative data in the first part of the locality file, and the data produced under the present heading. In practice, however, the more detailed data that are of relevance here might originate from sources different from those presented in the first part of the locality file. Observe that the notion of a leading activity may refer to either a prospering or a declining activity.

Economic indicators can also be produced (partly at least) for important firms. Such indicators would include employment and its different categories (female/male, qualifications, migrants, etc.) over a relatively long period; the same for output (main product categories, exports, imports), investments (local, inward, etc.), profits, and support from the public sector at its different spatial levels. They might possibly include prices, cost structure, indicators of competitive position.

2.5.3. Contemporary leading economic activities: qualitative economic indicators

Characterization of the economic activity: traditional, mature, informal, and innovative.

Explain the characterization using arguments about competitiveness (price and cost competitiveness, quality and innovative content of products, product life cycle, stage of innovation in production process, marketing strategy).

Relationships between the leading activities and other activities in and outside the region: the geography of the forward and backward linkages of the enterprises belonging to the leading activities.

Managerial traditions: business strategies, the organization and management style, the geographical linkages of managers, business culture (engineering, manufacturing, domestic or outward oriented, networking, service orientation, collaboration with unions, socio-professional organizations, etc.).

Institutional influences specific to the leading activities: labour unions, socio-professional organizations, work attitudes, work models (Taylorist, etc.), attitudes *vis-à-vis* unions and social struggle.

2.5.4. Leading economic activities and economic (dis)integration

The strategic meaning of the leading economic sectors for the development potential of the locality: the future of the sectors.

Integration in the local economic structure in the regional and national economy: investment and trade flows; the geography of the main capital groups' commuting and migration flows; involvement in wider area development strategies.

2.6. *Social reproduction dynamics in the locality*

2.6.1. Demography:

In and out migration;

In and out commuting: a qualitative interpretation of demographic and mobility data (see part I of locality file).

2.6.2. Class, family, and gender:

Socio-professional classification and composition of households;

Income situation; gender composition of households (interpretation of quantitative data in part I of locality file);

Qualitative appraisal of family culture.

2.6.3. Educational system: existing schools and educational programmes; qualitative appraisal.

2.6.4. Cultural institutions: churches, socio-cultural organizations and their impact on socio-economic attitudes and culture; role of artistic and intellectual creativity.

2.6.5. Characterization of community life.

This subsection is meant to give a comprehensive picture of group and movement life, socio-cultural images, locality culture, etc., as they exist in the locality.

2.7. *Social reproduction, the educational system, and the labour-market in relationship to leading economic activities*

The leading economic sectors are important employers. One can expect that they move the reproduction of the local labour force in different ways: (i) by their labour demand and employment. In this way they determine the professional reproduction of labour power

(overspecialization limiting access to other activities, polyvalent professional experience, impact on health and mind, etc.); (ii) by their expulsion of labour power: creating unemployment, with unequal chances for new employment among the unemployed; (iii) by influencing, directly or indirectly, parts of the schooling and training system; (iv) by exerting an impact on socio-cultural organizing, the development of local culture, social and work attitudes. This impact can be in conformity with the ideology of the leading firms, or in reaction against it.

Section 2.7 must therefore contain a summary of the different elements of the reproduction of labour power in interaction with the leading sectors.

2.8. Local planning or allocation in general/development initiatives/agencies

This should include local development dynamics, with a description of the supra-local agencies/institutions involved, and cover the formation of development action networks (re education and training, technology, strategy and organization, etc.).

2.8.1. Domains in which local development initiatives are taken:

> services: management and organization assistance, investment advice, fiscal advice, etc;
> services: logistics for new starters;
> technology transfer;
> investment funds;
> education and vocational (re)training—reskilling;
> industrial apprenticeship model;
> socio-cultural mobilization: developing business and social culture;
> R. & D.;
> industrial infrastructure;
> land;
> housing;
> collective consumption;
> tourism;
> infrastructure.

Indicate for which domains agents take initiatives in the locality; indicate also the forms of networking and collaboration.

2.8.2. Local development agents and their networks. Which development agents are active on the local scene now and in which collaborative forms?

> enterprises, public and/or private, and in which form of co-operation?
> public/private/mixed development corporations;
> regional–local partnerships;
> community–national–regional–local partnerships;
> autonomous development authorities.

Which are the main target areas/constituencies of these agents? Do the development strategies of these agents reach the most excluded segments of the local population? Which instruments do they use?

2.8.3. Evaluation of existing development agents, networks, and actions.

Which are considered as successful? Which are considered as a failure? Why? Develop arguments in terms of: objectives of development actions—partners involved—agencies put in place or mobilized—instruments and resources—mobilization of constituencies, economic, and social agents etc.

2.9. Perspectives for further development in the local community

This should cover new initiatives for co-operation between civil society, the business sector, and public authorities; and new links between economic, social, and cultural actions, etc.

BIBLIOGRAPHY

ACHTERHUIS, H. (1998), *De erfenis van de UTOPIE* (Amsterdam: Ambo).

AGLIETTA, M. (1976), *Régulation et crises du capitalisme* (Paris: Calmann-Lévy).

ALTVATER, E. (1993), *The Future of the Market: An Essay on the Regulation of Money and Nature after the Collapse of 'Actually Existing Socialism'* (London: Verso).

——(1997), 'Restructuring the Space of Democracy. The Effects of Capitalist Globalization and of the Ecological Crisis on Form and Substance of Democracy' (Paper presented at the International Academic Conference, Environmental Justice, Global Ethics for the 21st Century, University of Melbourne, Australia, 1–3 October).

AMIN, A., and ROBBINS, K. (1992), 'Le Retour des économies régionales? La géographie mythique de l'accumulation flexible', in G. Benko and A. Lipietz (eds.), *Les Régions qui gagnent. Districts et réseaux: les nouveaux paradigmes de la géographie économique (*Paris: Presses Universitaires de France).

——and THRIFT, N. (1995), 'Globalisation, Institutional "Thickness" and the Local Economy', in Patsy Healey *et al.* (eds.), *Managing Cities: The New Urban Context* (London: John Wiley), 91–108.

——and TOMANEY, J. (1995*a*) (eds.), *Behind the Myth of European Union* (London and New York: Routledge).

——and —— (1995*b*), 'The Regional Development Potential of Inward Investment in the Less Favoured Regions of the European Community', in A. Amin and J. Tomaney (eds.), *Behind the Myth of European Union* (London and New York: Routledge).

AMIN, S. (1970), *L'Accumulation à l'échelle mondiale* (Paris: Editions Anthropos).

——(1973), *Le Développement inégal. Essai sur les formes sociales du capitalisme périphérique* (Paris: Editions du Minuit).

——*et al.* (1982), *Dynamics of Global Crisis* (New York and London: Monthly Review Press).

ANELL, L. (1981), *Recession: The Western Economies and the Changing World Order* (London: Frances Pinter).

AUTÈS, M. (1997), 'Public Action, Local Democracy and the Challenge of Economic Globalization', in F. Moulaert and A. Scott (eds.), *Cities, Enterprises and Society on the eve of the 21st Century* (London: Pinter).

BAGNASCO, A. (1994), 'Regioni, tradizione civica, modernazzizazione italiana: un commento alla ricerca di Putnam', *Stato e Mercato*, 40.

——and TRIGIGLIA, C. (1993), *La Construction sociale du marché* (Paris: Presses ENS Cachan).

BENASSI, D., KAZEPOV, Y., and MINGIONE, E. (1997), 'Socio-Economic Restructuring and Urban Poverty under Different Welfare Regimes', in F. Moulaert and A. Scott (eds.), *Cities, Enterprises and Society on the Eve of the 21st Century* (London: Pinter).

BENKO, G., and LIPIETZ, A. (1992) (eds.), *Les Régions qui gagnent. Districts et réseaux: les nouveaux paradigmes de la géographie économique* (Paris: Presses Universitaires de France).

BINGHAM, R. D., and MIER, R. (1993), *Theories of Local Economic Development* (Newbury Park: Sage Publications).

BODSON, D., and HIERNAUX, J. P. (1981), *La Face cachée* (Bruxelles: Editions Vie Ouvrière).

BOOKCHIN, M. (1974), *The Limits of the City* (New York: Harper and Row).

BOYER, R. (1979), 'La Crise actuelle: une mise en perspective historique', *Critique de l'Economie Politique,* **7–8**: 5–112.

——(1986*a*) (ed.), *Capitalismes fin de siècle* (Paris: Presses Universitaires de France).

——(1986*b*), 'Segmentations ou solidarité, déclin ou redressement: Quel modèle pour l'Europe?', in R. Boyer (ed.), *Capitalismes fin de siècle* (Paris: Presses Universitaires de France).

——(1986*c*), *La Théorie de la régulation: Une analyse critique* (Paris: La Découverte).

——and MISTRAL, J. (1983), 'La Crise actuelle: d'une analyse historique à une vue prospective', *CEPREMAP couverture rouge* 8304.

——and ORLÉAN, A. (1990), 'La Convention salariale: les obstacles d'une innovation locale dans la transformation du mode de régulation', *CEPREMAP couverture rouge* 9029.

Brandt Commission, *Common Crisis* (London: Pan, 1983).

BRAUDEL, F. (1979), *Civilisation matérielle, économie et capitalisme, XVe–XVIIIe siècle,* ii. *Les Jeux de l'échange* (Paris: Armand Colin).

BROWN, A. J., and BURROWS, E. M. (1977), *Regional Economic Problems* (London: Allen and Unwin).

BRUSCO, S. (1982), 'The Emilian model: Productive Decentralisation and Social Integration', *Cambridge Journal of Economics,* **6**: 167–84.

——(1986), 'Small Firms and Industrial Districts: The Experience of Italy', in D. Keeble and E. Weaver (eds.), *New Firms and Regional Development in Europe* (London: Croom Helm).

BUCKINGHAM-HATFIELD, S., and EVANS, B. (1996) (eds.), *Environmental Planning and Sustainability* (Chichester: John Wiley).

CASSEL, Ph. (1993), *The Giddens Reader* (London: Macmillan).

CASTELLS, M. (1975), *Luttes urbaines* (Paris: Petite collection Maspero).

——(1983), *The City and the Grassroots* (Berkeley: The University of California Press).

CETTE, G., and TADDÉI, S. (1997), *Réduire la durée du travail. De la théorie à la pratique* (Paris: INEDIT).

Cocoyoc Declaration, *Development Dialogue,* **2**: 88–96 (Dag Hammarskjöld Foundation).

Commission Européenne (1991; 1992; 1993; 1994; 1995), *Rapport annuel sur la mise en oeuvre de la réforme des fonds structurels* (Brussels).

——(1994*a*), *Compétitivité et cohésion: tendances dans les régions. Cinquième rapport périodique sur la situation et l'évolution socio-économiques des régions de la communauté* (Brussels).

——(1994*b*), *Europe 2000+ Coopération pour l'aménagement du territoire européen* (Brussels).

——(1996), *Premier rapport sur la cohésion économique et sociale* (Brussels).

Commission of the European Communities (1991), *The Regions in the 1990s* (Brussels: CE, Directorate-General for Regional Policy).

COOKE, Ph. (1988), 'Flexible Integration, Scope Economies, and Strategic Alliances: Social and Spatial Mediations', *Society and Space,* **6**.

——(1989) (ed.), *Localities: The Changing Face of Urban Britain* (London: Unwin Hyman).

COOKE, Ph., MOULAERT, F., SWYNGEDOUW, E., and WEINSTEIN, O. (1992), *Towards Global Localization: The Computing and Communication Industries in Britain and France* (London: University College London Press).

CORIAT, B., and DOSI, G. (1995), 'Evolutionisme et régulation: différences et convergences', in R. Boyer and Y. Saillard, *La Théorie de la régulation. Etat des savoirs* (Paris: Presses Universitaires de France).

COX, K. (1995), 'Globalisation, Competition and the Politics of Local Economic Development', *Urban Studies*, **32**(2): 213–24.

——(1997), *Spaces of Globalization: Reasserting the Power of the Local* (New York and London: The Guilford Press).

CUYVERS, L., and RAYP, G. (1997), *Social Dumping and Social Competition in the Global Economy* (Antwerp University: RUCA).

DAVID, P. (1975), 'Clio and the Economics of QWERTY', *American Economic Review*, **75**: 332–7.

DE DECKER, P., HUBEAU, B., and NIEUWINCKEL, St. (1996) (eds.), *In de ban van stad en wijk* (Antwerp: EPO).

DEMAZIÈRE, Ch. (1997), 'Contribution au débat sur l'intégration de l'espace dans la théorie économique. Développement et crise d'une ville de tradition industrielle—Charleroi (Belgique)', *Espaces et Sociétés,* **88/89**: 184–206.

——(1998), *Développement économique et espace urbain* (Paris: Economica-Anthropos,1998).

DICKEN, P. (1994), 'Global–Local Tensions: Firms and States in the Global Space Economy', *Economic Geography,* **70**: 101–28.

DOSI, G. *et al.* (1988) (eds.), *Technical Change and Economic Theory* (London and New York: Pinter Publishers).

DOUTHWAITE, R. (1996), *Short Circuit: Strengthening Local Economies for Security in an Unstable World* (Foxhole: Green Books).

DRYZEK, J. S. (1999), 'Global Ecological Democracy' in N. Low ed. *Global Ethics and Environment* (London, Routledge).

DUNFORD, M., and KAFKALAS, G. (1992) (eds.), *Cities and Regions in the New Europe: The Global–Local Interplay and Spatial Development Strategies* (London: Belhaven).

EADE, J. (1997) (ed.), *Living the Global. Globalization as Local Process* (London and New York: Routledge).

EKINS, P. (1992), *A New World Order: Grassroots Movements for Global Change* (London and New York: Routledge).

ERASMUS (1515), *Praise of Folly,* trans. Betty Radice (London: Penguin).

European Foundation for the Improvement of Living and Working Conditions (1992), *Out of the Shadows. Local community action and the European Community* (Luxembourg: Official Publication of the European Community).

European Institute of Urban Affairs. *Urbanisation and the Functions of Cities in the European Community* (Brussels/Liverpool: EEC/Liverpool John Moores University).

FABER, D. (1998), 'The Political Ecology of American Capitalism: New Challenges for the Environmental Justice Movement', in D. Faber (ed.), *The Struggle for Ecological Democracy: Movements for Environmental Justice in the United States* (New York: Guilford Press).

FATHI, M. (1996), *L'Organisation du développement local et la réforme révisée des fonds structurels européens.* Mémoire de DEA (Economie Industrielle et des Ressources

Humaines. Lille, France: Université de Lille I, Faculté des Sciences Economiques et Sociales).

FEATHERSTONE, M., LASH, S., and ROBERTSON, R. (1995) (eds.), *Global Modernities* (London: Sage).

FEYERABEND, P. (1975), *Against Method* (London: New Left Books).

FISHER, R. (1993), 'Grass-Roots Organizing Worldwide: Common Ground, Historical Roots, and the Tension between Democracy and the State', in R. Fisher and J. Kling (eds.), *Mobilizing the Community: Local Politics in the Era of the Global City* (Thousand Oaks, Calif.: Sage Publications).

——and KLING, J. (1993) (eds.), *Mobilizing the Community: Local Politics in the Era of the Global City* (Thousand Oaks: Sage Publications).

Freie und Hansestadt Hamburg (1994), *Armutsbekämpfung in Hamburg* (Hamburg: Stadtentwicklungsbehörde).

FRIEDMANN, J. (1992), *Empowerment: The Politics of Alternative Development* (Cambridge, Mass., and Oxford: Blackwell).

GALLOUJ, F. (1994), *Economie de l'innovation dans les services* (Paris: Editions L'Harmattan).

GIBBS, D. (1996), 'Integrating Sustainable Development and Economic Restructuring: A Role for Regulation Theory?', *Geoforum*, **27**(1): 1–10.

GIBSON, A. B. (1969), *Muse and Thinker* (Harmondsworth: Penguin).

GIUNTA, A., and MARTINELLI, F. (1995), 'The Impact of Post-Fordist Corporate Restructuring in a Peripheral Region: the Mezzogiorno of Italy', in A. Amin and J. Tomaney (eds.), *Behind the Myth of European Union* (London and New York: Routledge).

GODELIER, M. (1972), *Rationality and Irrationality in Economics* (London and New York: Monthly Review Press).

GOODWIN, M., DUNCAN, S., and HALFORD, S. (1993), 'Regulation Theory, the Local State, and the Transition of Urban Politics', *Society and Space*, **11**: 67–88.

GOTTSCHALK, P., and SMEEDING, T. M. (1997), 'Cross-National Comparisons of Earnings and Income Inequality', *Journal of Economic Literature*, **35**: 633–87.

GRABHER, G. (1993) (ed.), *The Embedded Firm: On the Socio-economics of Industrial Networks* (London and New York: Routledge).

GRAVIER, J. F. (1949), *Mise en valeur de la France* (Paris: le Portulan).

HADJIMICHALIS, C., and VAIOU, D. (1990), 'Whose Flexibility? The Politics of Informalisation in Southern Europe', *Capital and Class,* **42**: 79–105.

Hammarskjöld Foundation (1975), *What Now?, Another Development* (Uppsala: DHF).

HÄNTSCH, U., and SCHMALRIEDE, K. (1996), 'Unemployment, Poverty and Social Exclusion in Hamburg' (Paper presented at the Lepu-Conference, London, 14 November).

HARLOE, M., PICKVANCE, Ch., and URRY, J. (1990) (eds.), *Place Policy and Politics: Do Localities Matter?* (London: Unwin Hyman).

HARVEY, D. (1973), *Social Justice and the City* (London: Edward Arnold).

——(1989), *The Condition of Postmodernity: An Enquiry into the Conditions of Cultural Change* (Cambridge, Mass.: Blackwell).

HÄUSSERMANN, H., *et al*. (1993*a*), 'Case Study on Hamburg' (EU, Poverty III Programme, Lille).

——*et al*. (1993*b*), 'Case Study on Rostock' (EU, Poverty III Programme, Lille).

HELD, D., MCGREW, A., GOLDBLATT, D., and PERRATON, J. (1999), *Global Transformations: Politics, Economics and Culture* (Cambridge: Polity Press).

HIRST, P., and THOMPSON, G. (1996), *Globalization in Question* (Cambridge: Polity Press).

HODGSON, G. (1988), *Economics and Institutions: A Manifesto for a Modern Institutional Economics* (Cambridge: Polity Press).

HOLLIS, M., and NELL, E. (1975), *Rational Economic Man: A Philosophical Critique of Neo-Classical Economics* (London: Cambridge University Press).

HYMER, S. (1972), 'The Multinational Corporation and the Law of Uneven Development', in J. N. Bhagwati (ed.), *Economics and the World Order* (London: Macmillan).

ICDSI (Independent Commission on Disarmament and Security Issues) (1982), *Common Security: A Programme for Disarmament* (London: Pan).

JESSOP, B. (1989), 'Regulation Theories in Retrospect and Prospect', *Economies et Sociétés*, **11**: 7–62.

——(1990), 'Regulation Theories in Retrospect and Prospect', *Economy and Society*, **19**: 153–216.

JONES, E. (1990), *Metropolis: The World's Great Cities* (Oxford: Oxford University Press).

KAZEPOV, Y., and ZAJCZYK, Fr. (1997), 'Urban Poverty and Social Exclusion: Concept and Debates', in F. Moulaert and A. Scott (eds.), *Cities, Enterprises and Society on the Eve of the 21st Century* (London and Washington: Pinter).

KEEBLE, D., and WEAVER, E. (1986) (eds.), *New Firms and Regional Development in Europe* (London: Croom Helm,1986).

——OFFORD, J., and WALKER, S. (1988), *Peripheral Regions in a Community of Twelve Member States* (Brussels: EEC).

KING, R. (ed.) (1993*a*), *Mass Migration in Europe: The Legacy and the Future* (London: Belhaven Press).

——(1993*b*), 'European International Migration 1945–1990: A Statistical and Geographical Overview', in R. King (ed.), *Mass Migration in Europe: The Legacy and the Future* (London: Belhaven Press).

KLEIN, J. L. (1997), 'L'Espace local à l'heure de la globalisation: la part de la mobilisation sociale', *Cahiers de Géographie du Québec,* **41**(114): 367–77.

——and LÉVESQUE, B. (1995), *Contre l'exclusion. Repenser l'économie* (Sainte Foy: Presses de l'Université du Québec).

——and TREMBLAY, P.A. (1997) (eds.), *Au delà du néolibéralisme. Quel rôle pour les mouvements sociaux?* (Sainte Foy: Presses de l'Université du Québec).

KRIFA, H., and MOULAERT, F. (1991), *Croissance externe, réorganisation fonctionnelle et localisation des grandes firmes multinationales* (Lille: IFRESI-CNRS).

LAMBOOY, J., and MOULAERT, F. (1996), 'The Economic Organisation of Cities: An Institutional Perspective', *International Journal of Urban and Regional Research*, **20**(2): 217–37.

LEBORGNE, D., and LIPIETZ, A. (1990), 'Fallacies and Open Issues about Post-Fordism', *Couverture Rouge* 9009 (Paris: CEPREMAP).

LE GALÈS, P. (1995), 'Du gouvernement des villes à la gouvernance urbaine', *Revue Française de Science Politique,* **45**(1): 57–95.

——(1998), 'Regulations and Governance in European Cities', *International Journal of Urban and Regional Research,* **22**(3): 482–506.

Leontidou, L. (1990), *The Mediterranean City in Transition* (Cambridge: Cambridge University Press).

Leroy, M. C. (1990), *Voyage dans 10 quartiers européens en crise* (Paris: L'harmattan).

Lipietz, A. (1977), *Le Capital et son espace* (Paris: Maspero).

——(1988), 'Reflections on a Tale: The Marxist Foundations of the Concepts of Regulation and Accumulation', *Studies in Political Economy*, **26**: 7–36.

——(1989), 'De l'althusserianisme à la théorie de la régulation', *Couverture Rouge* 8920 (Paris: CEPREMAP).

——(1992*a*), *Towards a New Economic Order: Postfordism, Ecology and Democracy* (Cambridge: Polity Press).

——(1992*b*), 'The Regulation Approach and Capitalist Crisis: An Alternative Compromise for the 1990s', in M. Dunford and G. Kafkalas (eds.), *Cities and Regions in the New Europe: The Global–Local Interplay and Spatial Development Strategies* (London: Belhaven).

Low, N. (1994), 'Growth Machines and Regulation Theory: The Institutional Dimension of the Regulation of space in Australia', *International Journal of Urban and Regional Research*, **18**: 451–69.

——and Gleeson, B. J. (1999), 'Global Governance for Environmental Justice', *Pacifica Review*, **11-2**: 177–93.

Marden, P. (1990), 'Modern Capitalist Society and a Theory of Regulation: Searching for the Elusive Archimedean Point' (Monash University, Department of Geography and Environmental Science, Working Paper No. 31).

Markusen, A. (1983), 'Regions and Regionalism', in F. Moulaert and P. Wilson (eds.), *Regional Analysis and the New International Division of Labor* (Boston: Kluwer Nijhoff).

Martens, A. (1977), 'De destructuratie van de arbeidsmarkt', *Sociologische Gids*, 1.

—— (1996), 'Bewonersparticipatie in de Brusselse Noordwijk', in P. De Decker *et al.*, *In de ban van stad en wijk* (Antwerp: EPO).

——and Vanden Eede, M. (1994), *De Noordwijk. Slopen en wonen* (Antwerpen: EPO).

Martinelli, F. (1988), *Productive Organization and Service Demand in Italian Textile and Clothing 'Districts': A Case Study* (Geneva: UNCTAD/MTN/RLA/CB.6).

——and Schoenberger, F. (1992), 'Oligopoly is Alive and Well: Notes for a Broader Discussion of Flexible Accumulation', in G. Benko and M. Dunford (eds.), *Industrial Change and Regional Development: The Transformation of New Industrial Spaces* (London: Belhaven Press).

Martínez, P. M., and Vicario, L. (1997), 'Polarización Socio-Espacial en el Area Metropolitana de Bilbao', *INGURUAK, Revista Vasca de Sociología y Ciencia Política*, April 1997 (Leioa: EHU-UPV).

Marynissen, R., Poppe, E., Jacobs, T., and Van Hove, E. (1987), *Kansarmoede in de Grootstad Antwerpen. Parts I + II: De Kwaliteit van het Wonen* (Antwerp: UIA and Fondation Roi Baudouin).

Massey, D. (1984), *Spatial Divisions of Labour: Social Structures and the Geography of Production* (London: Macmillan).

——(1996), 'Tension in the City: Between Anonymity and Danger', in A. Merriefield and E. Swyngedouw (eds.), *The Urbanization of Injustice* (London: Lawrence & Wishart).

Massey, D., Quintas, P., and Wield, D. (1992), *High Tech Fantasies: Science Parks in Society, Science and Space* (London and New York: Routledge).

MATTHEWS, J. (1996), 'Social Processes and the Pursuit of Sustainable Urban Development', in S. Buckingham-Hatfield and B. Evans (eds.), *Environmental Planning and Sustainability* (Chichester: John Wiley).

MAYER, M. (1995), 'Urban Restructuring, New Forms of Exclusion, and the Role of Social Movements' (Paper presented at the Acquafredda Conference, ESF/RC 23 of the International Sociological Association).

MINGIONE, E. (1991), *Fragmented Societies: A Sociology of Economic Life beyond the Market Paradigm* (Oxford: Basil Blackwell).

MOMMAAS, H. (1996), 'Modernity, Postmodernity and the Crisis of Social Modernization: A Case Study in Urban Fragmentation', *International Journal of Urban and Regional Research*, **20**(2): 196–216.

MOULAERT, F. (1987), 'An Institutional Revisit of the Storper-Walker Theory of Labor', *International Journal of Urban and Regional Research*, **11**(3): 309–30.

——(1993), 'Socio-Cultural Trajectories in Regional and Sub-Regional Development' (Paper presented at the 4th Seminar, Europe of the Cultures, Bruges, 26–7 November).

——(1996*a*), 'Measuring Socio-Economic Disintegration at the Local Level in Europe', in G. Room (ed.), *Beyond the Freshold: The Measurement and Analysis of Social Exclusion* (Bristol: Policy Press).

——(1996*b*), 'Rediscovering Spatial Inequality in Europe: Building Blocks for an Appropriate Regulationist Framework', *Society and Space*, **14**: 155–79.

——*et al.* (1990), *Integrated Area Development and Efficacy of Local Action*, study commissioned by the European Commission DG (Lille: IFRESI-CNRS).

——and DE CANNIÈRE, L. (1987), 'Income Inequality and Consumptive Spending Behavior: Empirical Evidence from the 1978–79 Budget Survey in Belgium', *Journal of Post Keynesian Economics*, **10**(2).

——and DELVAINQUIÈRE, J. C. (1994), 'Regional and Sub-Regional Trajectories in Europe: The Role of Socio-Cultural Innovation', in L. Bekemans (ed.), *Culture: Building Stone for Europe 2002* (Brussels: European Interuniversity Press).

——DELVAINQUIÈRE, J. C., and DELLADETSIMA, P. (1997), 'Rapports sociaux dans le développement local. Le rôle des mouvements sociaux', in J. L. Klein (ed.), *Au delà du néolibéralisme: quel rôle pour les mouvements sociaux?* (Sainte Foy: Presses Universitaires du Québec).

——and DEMAZIÈRE, Ch. (1996*a*), 'Local Economic Development in Post-Fordist Europe: Survey and Strategy Reflections', in C. Demazière and P. Wilson, *Local Economic Development in Europe and the Americas* (London: Mansell).

——and ——(1996*b*), 'Le Développement économique local dans une Europe Post-Fordiste', in C. Demazière and F. Moulaert, *Du local au global. Les initiatives locales pour le développement économique en Europe et en Amérique* (Paris: L'Harmattan).

——FARCY, H., DELVAINQUIÈRE, J. C., and DEMAZIÈRE, Ch. (1996), *La Métropole du Nord et son organisation économique. Une application des théories économiques institutionnelles à la régulation du développement économique local* (Lille/Paris: IFRESI-CNRS, Recherche pour le Plan Urbain).

——and LEONTIDOU, L. (1995), 'Localités désintégrées et stratégies de lutte contre la pauvreté: une réflexion méthodologique postmoderne', *Espaces et Sociétés*, **78**: 35–53.

——————DELLADETSIMA, P., DELVAINQUIÈRE, J. C., and DEMAZIÈRE, Ch. (1992, 1993, 1994*a*), *Local Development Strategies in Economically Disintegrated Areas: A Pro-Active Strategy against Poverty in the European Community,* Reports for the European Commission, DG V (Lille: IFRESI-CNRS).

——————————and ——(1994*b*), 'Propositions théoriques pour l'étude des localités qui "perdent"', in C. Courlet and B. Soulage (eds.), *Industrie, Territoires et Politiques Publiques* (Paris, L'Harmattan).

——SEKIA, F., and BOYABE, J. B. (1999), 'Innovative Region, Social Region? An Alternative View of Regional Innovation' (Lille: IFRESI-CNRS).

——and SHACHAR, A. (1995) (eds.), 'Globalization, Networks and Cities of Systems', *Urban Studies*, special issue **32**: 2.

——and SCOTT, A. (1997) (eds.), *Cities, Enterprises and Society on the Eve of the 21st Century* (London and Washington: Pinter).

——and SWYNGEDOUW, E. (1989), 'A Regulation Approach to the Geography of Flexible Production Systems', *Society and Space*, **7**: 327–45.

——and——(1991), 'Regional Development and the Geography of the Flexible Production System', in U. Hilpert (ed.), *Regional Innovation and Decentralization: High Tech Industry and Government Policy* (London and New York: Routledge).

——and——(1992), 'Accumulation and Organization in C&C Industries: A Regulationist Approach', in Ph. Cooke, F. Moulaert, E. Swyngedouw, O. Weinstein, and P. Wells, *Towards Global Localization: The Computing and Communication Industries in Britain and France* (London: University College London Press).

—————and RODRIGUEZ, A. (forthcoming) (eds.), *Urban Restructuring and Social Polarisation in the City*.

—————and WILSON, P. (1988), 'Spatial Responses to Fordist and Post-Fordist Accumulation and Regulation', *Papers of the Regional Science Association*, **64**: 11–23.

——and VANDENBROUCKE, F. (1983), 'Bestrijding van de werkloosheid: de bijdrage van Post-Keynesiaance economen', in W. Van Ryckeghem (ed.), *Macro-economics and Policy* (Alphen a/d Rijn: Kluwer).

——and WILLEKENS, F. (1984), 'Regional Industrial Policy in Belgium: Towards a New Economic Feudalism?', in H. Muegge, W. Stöhr, *et al.* (eds.), *International Economic Restructuring and Regional Community* (Aldershot: Avebury).

NIEUWINCKEL, St. (1996), 'Wijkontwikkeling in Antwerpen', in P. De Decker *et al.* (eds.), *In de ban van stad en wijk* (Antwerp: EPO), 229–48.

NOTERMANS, T. (1997), 'Social Democracy and External Constraints', in K. R. Cox, *Spaces of Globalization: Reasserting the Power of the Local* (New York and London: The Guilford Press).

OECD (1983), *L'Enseignement, le développement urbain et les initiatives locales* (Paris: OECD.

OHNET, J. M. (1996), *Histoire de la décentralisation française* (Paris: Le Livre de Poche).

O'HARA, Ph. (1998), 'Capital and Inequality in Today's World' in D. Brown (ed.) *Thorstein Veblen in the Twenty-First Century* (Cheltenham: Edward Elgar Publishing), 171–88.

PECK, J. (1996), *Work Place: The Social Regulation of Labor Markets* (New York: The Guilford Press).

——and TICKELL, A. (1991), 'Regulation Theory and the Geographies of Flexible Accumulation: Transitions in Capitalism, Transitions in Theory' (University of Manchester, School of Geography, SPA Working Paper 12, Manchester).

PECK, J., and TICKELL, A. (1992), 'Local Modes of Social Regulation? Regulation Theory, Thatcherism and Uneven Development', *Geoforum*, **23**(3): 347–63.

PERNA, T. (1904), *Lo sviluppo insostenibie* (Napoli: Liguore Editore).

——(1998), *Fair Trade* (Torino: Bollati Boringhieri).

POLANYI, K. (1944, 1957), *The Great Transformation: The Political and Economic Origins of Our Time* (Boston: Beacon Press).

POLEKAR (1985), *Het laboratorium van de crisis. Debat over een nieuwe maatschappelijke ordening* (Leuven: Kritak).

PRETECEILLE, E. (1997), 'Urban Economic Restructuring and Public Policy', in F. Moulaert and A. Scott (eds.), *Cities, Enterprises and Society on the Eve of the 21st Century* (London: Pinter).

PUTNAM, R. (1993), *Making Democracy Work: Civic Traditions in Modern Italy* (Princeton: Princeton University Press).

QUÉVIT, M. (1991) (ed.), *Regional Development Trajectories and the Attainment of the European Internal Market* (Louvain-la-neuve: GREMI-UCL).

RETI (Regions Européennes de Tradition Industrielle), various conference documents.

ROBERTSON, R. (1992), *Globalization: Social Theory and Global Culture* (London: Sage).

RODRIGUEZ, A., *et al.* (1994), 'Estudio del Mercado de Trabajo y de la Estructura Económica de Barakaldo (Ayuntamiento de Barakaldo. Unpublished document).

SACHTER, H. (1996), 'Les Mutations économiques dans le Nord Pas de Calais. Une approche régulationniste apporte-t-elle des éléments nouveaux?' (Lille: Paper presented at the FREVILLE conference, 23 March).

SASSEN, S. (1991), *The Global City: New York, London, Tokyo* (Princeton: Princeton University Press).

SCHOENBERGER, E. (1988), 'From Fordism to Flexible Accumulation: Technology, Competitive Strategies, and International Location', *Society and Space*, **6**.

SCHUBERT, A. (1995), 'Socio-Economic Develoment in Rostock' (Paper presented at the Antwerp Seminar on 'Social Integration and Local Development Strategies in European Cities').

——(1998), 'Kontinuität und Wandel in einer ostdeutschen Industrie-, Hafen- und Universitätsstadt: die Hansestadt Rostock in Europa der Zukunft (Hansestadt Rostock: Mimeo).

SHACHAR, A. (1997), 'Economic Globalization and Dynamics', in F. Moulaert and A. Scott (eds.), *Cities, Enterprises and Society on the Eve of the 21st Century* (London: Pinter).

STANBACK, Th., and NOYELLE, Th. (1982), *Cities in Transition* (Osmun Totowa, NJ: Allanheld).

STORPER, M., and SCOTT, A. (1989), 'The Geographical Foundations and Social Regulation of Flexible Production Complexes', in J. Wolch and M. Dear (eds.), *The Power of Geography: How Territory Shapes Social Life* (Boston: Unwin Hyman).

——and WALKER, R. (1983), 'The Theory of Labor and the Theory of Location', *International Journal of Urban and Regional Research*, **7**(1): 1–43.

SUAREZ-VILLA, L., and ROURA, J. R. C. (1992), 'Regional Economic Integration and the Evolution of Disparities', *Papers in Regional Science*, **72**(4): 369–87.

SWYNGEDOUW, E. (1989), 'The Heart of the Place: The Resurrection of Locality in an Age of Hyperspace', *Geografiska Annaler*, **71B**(1): 31–42.

——(1992), 'Territorial Organization and the Space/Technology Nexus', *Transactions of the Institute of British Geographers*, **17**: 417–33.

THRIFT, N. (1989), 'New Times and Spaces? The Perils of Transition Models. Editorial', *Society and Space*, **7**: 127–30.

——(1994), 'Globalisation, Regulation, Urbanisation: The Case of Netherlands', *Urban Studies*, **31**: 365–80.

TOPALOV, C. (1989), 'A History of Urban Research: The French Experience since 1965', *International Journal of Urban and Regional Research*, **13**(4): 625–51.

VAN BERKEL, R. (1997), 'Urban Integration and Citizenship: Local Policies and the Promotion of Participation', in M. Roche and R. van Berkel (eds.), *European Citizenship and Social Exclusion* (Aldershot: Averbury).

VANDENBROUCKE, F. (1998), *Globalization, Inequality and Social Democracy* (London: IPPR).

VAN DEN EEDE, M., and MARTENS, A. (1994), *De Noordwijk. Slapen en wonen* (Antwerp: EPO).

VAN DOREN, P. (1996), 'Adopting the Innovative Environment Approach: A Programme of Regional Development for Charleroi', in Ch. Demazière and P.A. Wilson (eds.), *Local Economic Development in Europe and the Americas* (London: Mansell).

VEBLEN, T. (1899), *The Theory of the Leisure Class: An Economic Study of Institutions* (New York: Macmillan).

WALLERSTEIN, I. (1979), *The Capitalist World Economy* (Cambridge: Cambridge University Press).

WILSON, P., MOULAERT, F., and DEMAZIÈRE, Ch. (1997), 'Urban Restructuring and Local Response', in F. Moulaert and A. Scott (eds.), *Cities, Enterprises and Society on the Eve of 21st Century* (London: Pinter).

WOLCH, J. R., and LAW, R. (1989), 'Social Reproduction in a Post-Fordist Era. Editorial', *Society and Space*, **7**: 249–52.

World Commission on Environment and Development (WCED) (1987), *Our Common Future* (Oxford: Oxford University Press).

INDEX OF AUTHORS

SUBJECT INDEX